Other books written by Barry H. Harrin:

"A Manager's Guide to Guerrilla Warfare,"

"Guess Who's Listening at the Other End of Your Telephone"

"The Islamic Conquest of Europe 2020."

Helena Texas

The Toughest Town On Earth

Barry H. Harrin

M.S. Hollis, Artist, on the Cover.

Published By Comanche Press
Copyright © 2010 Barry Harrin

FIRST EDITION
Copyright © 2010
By Barry H. Harrin
Published in the United States of America
By Comanche Press
906 Lightstone Drive, San Antonio Texas 78258
Email: comanchepress@gmail.com
Website: www.helenatexas.com
ALL RIGHTS RESERVED
ISBN   978-0-9626012-3-1

Library of Congress Control Number: 2010916661

This book is dedicated to my sons, Brian and Brandon Harrin, without whose assistance and encouragement, this book would never have been written.

Preface

Not to know what happened before one was born is to always remain a child.

--Cicero

If you're like me, you've seen a lot of Hollywood westerns with stars like Gary Cooper, John Wayne and Clint Eastwood. However, one movie stands out from the rest and epitomizes the violence and danger of the old west.

That movie was "Gunfight at the O.K. Corral" and it took place in Tombstone, Arizona. The over-dramatic Hollywood version was a shootout between the law and the lawless - the essence of good versus evil ... Hollywood style.

Well let me tell you something friend, if you think Tombstone was a tough place, than you're in for a rude awakening when you learn the hidden story of Helena, Texas ... previously known as "the toughest town on earth."

Acknowledgments

First I would like to reiterate my gratitude to my sons Brian and Brandon Harrin. They spent many hours digging up artifacts in the blazing hot Texas summers, or helping me over many years to do research in libraries and dirty old buildings ... to find missing pieces of the puzzle.

I would also like to thank the members of the Karnes County Historical society, especially Sue Butler Carter, Elizabeth Taylor, Trip Ruckman and of course Ramona Noone, curator of the Karnes County Museum in Helena, Texas.

Naturally, I would like to thank the foremost Historian of South Texas, Robert Thonhoff, for his generosity in sharing his time and amazing knowledge with me and my sons. He certainly brought new interest to my sons after informing them that one of their ancestors Jose de Urrutia had been the Spanish military commander in San Antonio in the early 1700's.

I would like to also thank Lawrence Leibowitz and Martha Humphrey for editing the book and providing solid advice and Sue Hollis for her original painting used as our book cover. My thanks also go out to Tom Rifleman, Charlotte Nichols, Elmo Brockman and the late Tom and Shirley Ruckman for sharing their time and knowledge.

Introduction

This book is not meant to be a scholarly, politically correct or "white washed" version of history about Helena, about Texas or about the United States. My main objective was to bring to life "real history," utilizing the best original sources where ever possible.

Some of the history brought forth in this book may surprise or shock you, if that's the case, then I am happy. I say this because much of the history we are taught in school is boring, filtered and controlled by an eastern establishment group of historians and textbook publishers. This group has a set agenda and tends to filter out anything that doesn't fit their world view. As a result we and our children don't often get the "true history."

I began my research for this book in 1988. During that time I have read and analyzed hundreds of books, and documents. The vast majority of these repeat the same history, virtually word for word, showing the same pictures and documents repeatedly. In this book, you may see some of those same pictures and documents when absolutely necessary, but be assured you will see documents, information and pictures that are totally unique to this book.

It is my hope and desire that after reading this book, you and your children will truly understand how we got to where we are today both in the United States and particularly in Texas.

Table of Contents

Chapter 1: The Beginning of the End

It was one o'clock in the afternoon on the 26th of December in the year 1884. The sky was cold, dark and ominous, as freezing rain and sleet pounded the wooden structures and sidewalks of Helena, Texas. The streets were ankle deep in mud as the false wooden building fronts swayed and creaked with each bone chilling, icy gust of wind.

It was the day after Christmas and the locals were either recovering from celebrations or trying to stay warm to avoid the miserable weather that had struck Helena on Christmas Eve.

Some of the good citizens were huddled around their fireplaces or close to hot wood stoves. The other townspeople continued their post Christmas celebrations with loud whiskey charged voices at one of the 13 saloons[1] that had sprouted up like mushrooms after summer rainstorms.

For weeks rumors had swirled around town about the bad blood between Sheriff Edgar Leary and William Green Butler (WGB). Butler was the richest rancher in Karnes County. He and his family were furious that Sheriff Leary and his deputies had forced their way into the Butler mansion while Butler was driving his cattle towards Kansas on the Chisholm Trail. The sheriff even had the gall to storm into Butler's daughter's bedroom, tearing off her covers.

Sheriff Leary's excuse for the home invasion was to question Butler's 20 year old son Emmett who, the sheriff claimed, was wanted for questioning in connection with the murder of a Negro in Wilson County.

Word reached Helena in the morning that Emmett Butler and his sidekick Hugh McDonald were drunk, shooting and terrorizing the Polish town of Panna Maria six miles down the road from Helena. Rumors swirled from house to house and saloon to saloon that Emmett was coming to town to avenge the Butler home invasion by Sheriff Leary and his deputies.

At about one o'clock in the afternoon galloping horses could be heard above the howling wind, driving rain and sleet. A multitude of bobbing heads peeked out from behind drawn curtains or above swinging saloon doors.

Two mounted men in yellow rain slickers could be seen charging into town with water shooting off their bodies. As was the custom in old Helena, most of the 500[2] citizens were well armed including Sheriff Leary and his deputies.

Everything occurred so quickly it was hard for people to truly recollect what actually happened. One thing is certain. As soon as Emmett Butler and his sidekick dismounted and drunkenly tied up their horses, the sheriff and his deputies approached the two and demanded that they surrender their guns. Emmett's sidekick quickly complied. Emmett whirled around and pulled his six shooter, which was hidden under his rain slicker.[3] In the blink of an eye, a flame shot from his pistol and a large bullet slammed into the sheriff's chest at heart level.

As the sheriff slumped to the wooden sidewalk, blood gushing from his mortal chest wound, he gasped "He has killed me. Shoot him!"

Emmett's sidekick was quickly knocked to the ground by a mob of angry men as Emmett jumped on his horse and began to gallop out of town. Unfortunately for him, before he got half a block, what sounded like a gatling gun echoed throughout the town.

More than forty shots were fired at Emmett by the townspeople,[4] some of them slamming into his body and opening his brain to the freezing rain. As he lay moaning and bleeding on the ground, the populace all came out to see the arrogant rich man's son receive his just reward. Emmett was pronounced dead that evening.

Upon hearing this terrible news, William G. Butler cut short his cattle drive and raced home to gather up 25 of his heavily armed ranch hands. They rode into Helena to retrieve Emmett's body and to find out who shot his son.

When the 25 rough looking cowboys reached Helena not a soul could be seen or heard. William Butler yelled at the top of his lungs "I want to know who killed my son". All he heard was the sound of silence. He repeated this several times, his booming voice echoing back from the battered buildings. The only reply he got was the wind blowing sagebrush over the wooden sidewalks.

Receiving no human reply, William Butler roared "This town killed my son; now I'm going to kill this town."[5]

Figure 1 Grave of Emmett Butler in Kenedy, Texas Courtesy Sue Carter

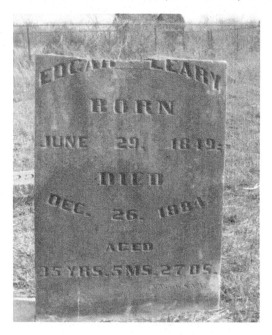

Figure 2 Grave of Sheriff Edgar Leary in Helena, Texas Courtesy Brian Harrin

Chapter 2: The Beginning

Since time immemorial, before the dinosaurs roamed through what is now South Texas, Karnes County and the town of old Helena were wild and violent places.

The low rolling hills, knee-high prairie grass and open rangeland, had always been a natural trail for man and beast to reach the sea.

After the reign of the dinosaur ended, Neanderthal man followed by hunter gatherer Native Americans roamed this area, first as prey and then as predator.

Ice age mammoths, native camels, giant sloths followed by black panthers, saber-tooth cats, giant bear, buffalo, deer and every size and type of snake slithered throughout this land.[6]

The ancient Indian trade routes were like a giant magnet. They attracted thousands of Indians from below the Rio Grande in the area now known as Chihuahua and Coahuila in northeastern Mexico to trade, raid and hunt.

There is an abundance of archeological evidence that the area currently known as Karnes County had been the site of human habitation for thousands of years before the arrival of Europeans.[7]

In the time before the arrival of Europeans, the future Karnes County was lush with vegetation and teeming with game. It became the hunting grounds for a number of tribes such as the Tonkawa, Karankawa and later the Comanche and Lipan Apache Indians.

Chapter 3: The Europeans Are Coming

The first Europeans to enter present-day Texas were the Spanish explorers. They arrived only a few years after the voyages of Christopher Columbus.

It began with Pineda sailing along the Texas coast in 1519 and continued with the exploration of the interior by the explorers Cabeza de Vaca during the period of 1528 to 1534. While seeking food sources, Cabaza de Vaca and his men may have been the first Europeans to pass through present day Karnes County and Helena. Another famous Spanish explorer in Texas was Coronado in the year 1541. He was followed by a multitude of Spanish explorers who wisely used Indian guides and ancient Indian trails, some of which appear to have passed through Karnes County and Helena area.[8]

These explorations brought some of the initial contacts between the Europeans and Native Americans and were the basis for Spain's claim on Texas. During this period there were many Native American tribes and cultures in the region. The Coahuiltecan, Karankawa, Caddo, Jumano and Tonkawa Indians lived in the area of present day Karnes County. Later the Apache and Comanche arrived.[9] Finally in 1718, Governor Martin de Alarcon led an expedition into Texas under the imperial banner of Spain. This is the first recorded history of Europeans in this territory.

At this time Spain was the leading superpower in the world and needed money to fight wars to maintain its superpower status. The Spanish empire was one of the largest in world history and one of the first global powers. Therefore, its primary motivation for exploration was the search for gold and silver to fill the royal treasury. This would provide the fuel to run its war engine and support its preeminent status.

Upon failing to acquire an abundance of gold and silver, its secondary goal became the capture of the Indians as cheap labor or their subsequent sale as slaves to raise money.

The French were the next to arrive in the late 1600s. The French came primarily as traders and many of them married and settled among some East Texas Native American tribes.

The Spanish and French were like time travelers from the future. The effect they had on the primitive Native Americans' culture was instantaneous, dramatic and permanent.

These Europeans introduced the Indians to futuristic trade goods such as guns and gunpowder, axes and knives, metal cooking utensils, blankets and cloth.[10] Naturally the introduction of these goods changed the way Native Americans went to war, hunted, or prepared their food, and dress.

There were two other important gifts the Europeans brought to Texas. The first was the Spanish introduction of domesticated horses. These were acquired by various Native American tribes who mastered their use in warfare. In fact, the Comanche's became the masters of mounted warfare and the best light cavalry in the world.

The second and most devastating gift presented by the Europeans to the Native American population of Texas and the rest of the Americas was disease. The Europeans brought smallpox, measles, whooping cough, cholera and, of course, the gift that keeps on giving ... syphilis.

These plagues spread throughout the Native American population like a forest fire. Indigenous people had little or no resistance to such virulent killers. The effect was overwhelming as they spread from village to village and from tribe to tribe.

There are conflicting estimates and disputes regarding the true size of the Native American population before the arrival of the Europeans. Surprisingly some experts have estimated that there were between 70 and 100 million[11] Native Americans in the new world before Columbus arrived, compared to Europe's population of 70 million.[12]

Although there is some question regarding the overall Native American population, what is less in dispute is the fact that millions of Indians were wiped out and the level of devastation and death rate may have been as high as a 90%.[13]

As an example: In 1521 just weeks before the famous conquistador, Hernan Cortes, seized control of Tenochtitlan (Mexico City), his military forces were on the verge of defeat. The Aztecs had continuously beaten back the Spanish invaders and were preparing a final offensive against them. Strangely, the attack never came. The weakened Spanish had their prayers answered by getting an unexpected chance to regroup. Cortes and his forces stormed the city on Aug. 21 only to find that some higher power had done their work for them. "I solemnly swear that all the houses and stockades in the lake were full of heads and corpses."

Cortez's chronicler, Bernal Diaz, wrote of the scene. "It was the same in the streets and courts ... we could not walk without treading on the bodies and heads of dead Indians. Indeed the stench was so bad that no one could endure it. ... and even Cortes was ill from the odors which assailed his nostrils. The same scent followed the Spaniards throughout the Americas.[14]

Clearly, the European conquest of North America and Mexico would have been much more difficult, if not impossible, had the Native Americans not been decimated by these diseases.

The actions of European invaders varied between the capture, enslavement, conversion or ethnic cleansing of the Native Americans. The bottom line is that exposure to Europeans devastated the indigenous cultures.[15]

Chapter 4: El Fuerte Del Cibolo

The failure of the Spanish to find gold and silver in Texas led them to lose interest in this region for more than a hundred years. However, Spain's interest level increased dramatically after France made an aggressive move in what they perceived as Spanish territory.

Tensions increased dramatically in the early 1680s after the famous French explorer La Salle claimed lands for France that included Texas. This was followed up by the arrival of La Salle with almost 300 French colonists and soldiers in Matagorda Bay and the construction of Fort St. Louis in what is now Victoria County, Texas. When word of this French invasion reached Mexico and the Spanish Government, Spain's interest level exploded and approached a national hysteria.[16]

To counter the invasion by La Salle and his French forces, the Spanish government sent various expeditions, by both land and sea, to locate them. However, these initial excursions were not to be successful. The Spanish had been unaware that in 1687: French explorer La Salle had been murdered in central East Texas by mutinous members of his own expedition.[17]

Around 1688 Governor Alonso de Leon of Coahuila captured a Frenchman, Jean Gery, in what is now Eagle Pass. After a strong interrogation, he agreed to lead de Leon and his party to locate the French Fort - Fort St. Louis.

Finally, in 1689 the Spanish Crown gave Governor Alonzo de Leon a commission to make an entrada (expedition) into Texas utilizing a number of soldiers, Indian guides, missionaries and, of course, the Frenchman Gery.[18]

This expedition began in Monclova (Coahuila) continued to Guerrero then crossed the Rio Grande at a river ford located about five miles from Guerrero. He first traveled to the northwest than went in a west southwesterly direction. He crossed South Texas coming close to such present day cities as Crystal City, Pearsall, Jourdanton, Karnes City/Helena, and Cuero continuing along Garcitas Creek until reaching a site near Matagorda Bay.

The French fort was found mostly destroyed and its inhabitants massacred. The cannibalistic Karankawa coastal Indians were believed to have been responsible for the massacre. Before reaching the fort, Governor de Leon had located several Indian camps and noted French muskets and missionary robes from the fort.[19]

The Karankawa were one of the more frightening tribes to the Europeans and to other Native American tribes. At this time, they primarily lived along the Texas coast between present Galveston Island and Corpus Christi.

The word Karankawa translated from their language means "dog-lovers" or "dog-raisers." That made sense since they reportedly kept dogs that were described as a fox-like or coyote-like breed. They hunted with huge bows almost as tall as they were and their arrows were said to be about 3 feet in length ... and deadly accurate and powerful.[20]

The Karankawa were the giants of their time, sometimes reaching almost 7 feet tall, while the typical European invader might average only 5 feet 5 inches. The Karankawa have been described as hideous looking by their enemies. Semi-naked or naked giants, faces and bodies were fully adorned with tattoos. They smelled awful ... probably due to the alligator grease and putrid mud they smeared from head to foot as a defense against mosquitoes. They were obnoxious to all observers.

There were many unpleasant reports from the Spanish and French who had first come into contact with the tribe. It appears that the Karankawa had a nasty habit after they captured their enemies. First the victim was tied, and then a fire was started as the Karankawa danced, leaped and yelled. The Karankawa then cut off their victims' body pieces; half roasted them in the fire and ate their flesh with great joy. This unpleasant ritual was completed by cutting off their victims scalp, attaching it to a pole as a trophy at their next communal dance.

It is believed that these acts of Cannibalism were to prevent the victim from having a second or third life. The Karankawa believed that whoever consumed their enemy absorbed their enemy's courage, and fighting skills. This must have been the ultimate revenge, to devour an enemy's flesh while he ... watched in complete terror.[21]

The Karankawa's ferocious appearance, smell, and cannibalistic tendencies brought fear and terror to all who visited them, so much so, that they wanted to avoid seeing the natives again. By the year 1860, on the eve of the American Civil War, the Karankawa had been completely exterminated.

In order to counter the French threat and convert the Caddo Indians to Christianity the Spanish built missions in east Texas around 1690. The area became a province of Spain by 1722, with settlements at San Antonio de Bexar (San Antonio) and the Presidio of La Bahia (moved to present-day Goliad in 1749).

The first Spanish settlement in the area started in San Antonio in 1718 and received a jump start in 1731 with the arrival of Spaniards from the Canary Islands, located off the coast of Africa. However, no real settlement occurred until after the first Spanish private grants were issued for the present Karnes County in 1758.

The first of these land grants were issued to Andrés Hernández and Luis Antonio Menchaca. Hernandez received the eastern section of land between the San Antonio River and Cibolo Creek known as El Rincon (the corner). Menchaca received the western section.

The San Antonio River Valley extending from San Antonio de Béxar (San Antonio) through the present Karnes County to La Bahía (now Goliad). It was the backbone of ranchos and the Spanish cattle industry. It was an area rich in rolling grasslands perfect for raising cattle. The original Spanish ranchos that flourished in the future Karnes County were the beginning of the huge American ranching industry.[22]

As these ranches began to multiply and grow, their large herds of long horn cattle became vital to the support of the missions in San Antonio and Goliad. Unfortunately, these ranches and their large herds of longhorn cattle became magnets attracting continuous raids by attacking Apaches.

The Governor of Texas Manuel de Sandoval decided to bolster defenses and provide greater security for these vital resources. To carry out this plan, his military commander, Jose de Urrutia,[23] the Captain of the San Antonio de Bexar Presidio implemented a plan of action for protection of these vital resources.

Jose de Urrutia had been in the new world since before 1691 and was considered the foremost Indian expert of his time. He spent seven years as a captive of the Indians and ultimately had 40 years experience either fighting or dealing with them. He had been "Captain General" of all nations hostile to the Apaches and conducted several extensive campaigns against them.[24]

Governor Sandoval and Urrutia ordered additional soldiers for the Presidio and positioned the herds at a remote site to protect their horses from the Indian raiders.

In 1734 a small fort called El Fuerte de Santa Cruz del Cibolo, El Fuerte del Cibolo, or Arroyo del Cíbolo or El Cíbolo was built there and a small garrison of soldiers were posted there. The site was at the natural ford on Cibolo Creek halfway between Béxar and La Bahía (~ 10 miles from present day Helena). This place was known by local residents as Carvajal Crossing (where present Farm Road 887 crosses Cibolo Creek in Karnes County).[25]

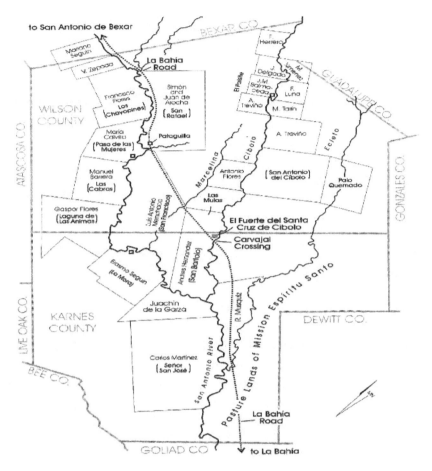

Figure 3 Map-Courtesy of Robert H. Thonhoff

This small fort is believed to have consisted of structures made of mud and sticks (jacales) and a few dugouts. It was abandoned in 1737 after only three years as a result of two devastating raids by the Apaches that resulted in the loss of more than 400 horses. The remaining soldiers and herds were moved back to San Antonio.

Although the Indian threat continued, more ranches were established as the mission road filled with traffic. In the vicinity of the outpost, Andres Hernandez established the first privately owned ranch in Texas.

In 1771, after the Spanish Colonial Government decided to increase frontier protection, the fort was re-established on the Cibolo near the site of present Czestochowa. This time the fort was of more substantial construction built with a wooden stockade so the local ranchers could seek shelter inside during Indian attacks. Over a 10 year period the fort and the garrisoned soldiers provided protection for the area ranches and the mail route between the Presidio la Bahia and San Antonio de Bexar (through present day Helena).

Attacks and hostilities with the Comanche's increased dramatically by 1782, when the fort closed again. This time the buildings were burned to prevent their use by the Comanche's. A number of ranches were abandoned, leaving less than a 100 settlers and only 6 or 7 ranches still operating.[26]

It was not until the early 1800s that the area gradually became repopulated. Eventually the enormous original ranches belonging to Hernández and Menchaca were divided up by heirs of the families. Subsequently, some of the land was sold to other families. These families included the Veramendi, Cassiano, Flores, Navarro, and Carillo clans, to name a few.[27]

In spite of the ranching activity, possibly due to Indian attacks, Texas remained a sparsely populated border frontier on the outer reaches of New Spain. Almost three hundred years after the Spanish first explored this area of Texas, the number of settlers had not exceeded 3,000.

Chapter 5: The American Revolution and Texas

When we study the American Revolution in school what do we learn? Well, most of the time we learn that the thirteen English colonies revolted against their mother country, England. They fought and struggled against overwhelming odds but, with the assistance of France; they defeated England and won their independence.

Guess what? That's not the whole story. Without the significant contribution of Spain and Texas we might not have won the American Revolution well over 200 years ago. A key part of that story is the critical role of Texas—its Hispanic soldiers, ranchers and citizens—and their contribution to winning the American war for independence.[28]

Most major historians have chosen to limit or totally ignore the significant contribution that both Spain and Texas Hispanics made to help us win our freedom. Most of our history books have been written or influenced by historians from the northeast, and these educators seem to be predisposed to favor the northern European countries over the Latin countries and their people.

Here are two examples:

(1)   It is a rare textbook or school that teaches students the actual size of Spain's holdings in North America. When the American Revolution began Spain either owned or claimed the entire North American continent west of the Mississippi River including Alaska and the New Orleans portion of Louisiana[29]

(2)   Very few of us learned in school that the Spanish Colonization of what became the United States actually began in 1598. This was nine years before the English established the first settlement at Jamestown and twenty-two years before the pilgrims landed at Plymouth Rock. This does not appear to be common knowledge in our school system.

We have been taught that the European heroes of the American Revolution had names such as Lafayette and Rochambeau (France), Von Steuben and de Kalb (Prussia), Pulaski and Kosciusko (Poland).

An unknown hero of the American Revolution was Bernardo de Galvez who served as the commander of the Spanish military and naval campaign against the British in North America.[30]

Bernardo de Galvez was born near Malaga, Spain in 1746. He came from an aristocratic and distinguished family of ancient nobility. He chose a military career like his father and uncle and served in the service of the King of Spain, Carlos III.

Galvez arrived in Mexico in 1765 and by 1769 he was sent to the northern frontier of New Spain. There he became second in command under Lope de Cuellar, commandant of the army of Nueva Vizcaya (The modern Mexican states of Chihuahua, Durango, and, parts of Sinaloa, Sonora, and Coahuila).

Galvez earned a reputation as a fierce warrior during a number of successful military campaigns along the Pecos and Gila rivers against the Apaches after they had caused great economic damage to the Spanish settlers.

In one of Galvez's battles, he became separated from his men and ran into five fierce enemy Indians. Single-handed he fought his way back to his men. He received an arrow in the arm and wounds in his chest from two lance thrusts. It would be a year before he recovered from his severe injuries.[31]

Gálvez returned to Spain in 1772. He was then sent to France for three years, studying military science, French language and culture. He returned to Spain in 1775 and served as captain of infantry under Alejandro O'Reilly in the Regiment of Seville. He was involved in a failed attack on Algiers and suffered another wound. As a result, he was promoted to the rank of lieutenant colonel and attached to the Military School of Ávila. In 1776 his life was to be changed forever. He was transferred to the faraway province of Louisiana and promoted to colonel of the Louisiana Regiment. On January 1, 1777, he succeeded Luis de Unzaga as governor of Louisiana.[32]

Gálvez provided significant assistance and did much to aid the American cause well in advance of Spain's entry in the American Revolutionary War. He wrote directly to key figures such as Patrick Henry, Thomas Jefferson and Charles Henry Lee and personally met with their representatives such as Oliver Pollock and Capt. George Gibson.[33]

Gálvez prevented the English from using the port of New Orleans. Under Galvez's leadership only American, French and Spanish ships were allowed the use of the Mississippi River. The river had become a critical lifeline for the American forces as military supplies, ammunition and large sums of money were delivered to the beleaguered forces of George Washington and George Rogers Clark.

Gálvez had waited patiently and finally on June 21, 1779 Spain made a formal declaration of war against Great Britain. The King of Spain, Carlos III then authorized Gálvez to secure a force of men and begin military operations against the British along the Mississippi River and the Gulf Coast.

Gálvez needed to feed his troops and to this end contacted Texas Governor Domingo Cabello y Robles. Galvez requested the transport of Texas cattle to Spanish forces in Louisiana. Between 1779 and 1782, 10,000 cattle were rounded up on Texas ranches belonging to missions and citizens of Bexar (San Antonio), La Bahía (Goliad) and the San Antonio River Valley.[34]

These massive herds of cattle were gathered at the Presidio (Fort) La Bahia and driven by vaqueros (cowboys) to Nacogdoches, Natchitoches and Opelousas to feed Galvez's soldiers.

Protection for the cattle drive was provided by soldiers from Presidio San Antonio de Béxar, Presidio La Bahía, and El Fuerte del Cíbolo (near present day Helena). Hundreds of horses were also brought along to support artillery and cavalry units.

19

In the fall of 1779, well fed on Texas beef, 1,400 Spanish soldiers defeated the British in battles at Manchac, Baton Rouge and Natchez. Galvez with 2000 soldiers and sailors captured the British stronghold of Fort Charlotte at Mobile on March 14, 1780.[35]

Galvez, the following year, commanded a joint land-sea attack on Pensacola which was then the British capital of West Florida. During the two-month siege, Galvez was in command of a force of more than 7,000 men including part of the French fleet, resulting in the capture Pensacola on May 10, 1781[36]

Galvez and the Spanish forces also wreaked havoc on the British by securing the upper Mississippi and Ohio Rivers. During the North American Campaign of the American Revolution the Spanish forces defeated the British in every battle.

The war was not confined to the North American continent. Spain battled the British in far off places like the Philippines, Galápagos, Honduras, Guatemala, Nicaragua, Bahamas, Jamaica, Minorca, and Gibraltar, as the Spanish and French continuously threatened an invasion of Great Britain itself.

In addition to Spanish troops Gálvez had under his command forces from Mayorca, Cuba, Puerto Rico, Hispaniola, Mexico (New Spain) Ireland, Louisiana Frenchmen, Germans, Acadians, Canary Islanders, Indians, black slaves and freedmen. In addition Galvez commanded a contingent of the American First Continental Marines and units from the South Carolina Navy.

Before peace negotiations ended the war on May 8, 1782, Galvez's forces, with support from the South Carolina Navy, captured the British naval base at New Providence in the Bahamas.

Once the fighting ended Gálvez participated in drafting the terms of the treaties that ended the war with the British Empire and established the boundary between Florida and the United States. Not long after this Gálvez was cited by the American Congress for his critical assistance during the war for independence.

After the peace accords in April 1783 General Gálvez returned to Spain with his family for a brief rest. In October 1784, he was recalled to America to serve as captain-general and governor of Cuba. In February 1785, Gálvez went to Savannah and then Baltimore to represent Spain in negotiations with the United States concerning the boundary between Florida and the United States.

Galvez was in Havana, Cuba in April when he learned that his father, Matías de Gálvez, had died on November 3, 1784 and that he had been appointed as Viceroy of New Spain replacing his father.

In June of 1785 Gálvez and his family arrived in Mexico City to begin his duties as Viceroy of New Spain. Gálvez the gallant Spanish hero and great supporter of American independence died of an illness on November 30, 1786.[37]

Chapter 6: The Battle of Medina

The first Anglo-American settlers began arriving in Texas in the early 19th century. At this time Texas was part of Mexico and still owned and controlled by Spain. During this period there were a number of attempts to achieve independence and freedom from Spanish rule.[38]

One of the most significant attempts was the battle of Medina fought on August 18, 1813 between the Republican forces of the Gutiérrez-Magee expedition under Gen. José Álvarez de Toledo y Dubois and a Spanish Royalist Army under Gen. Joaquín de Arredondo.[39]

This was a chaotic period in world history. Spain's time as a world superpower was quickly running out. The Battle of Medina (near present day San Antonio, Texas) had a dramatic affect on the future of France, England, Spain, Mexico and the United States.

Spain's king, Joseph Bonaparte was facing revolts in Latin America and Mexico as his brother, Napoleon terrorized the European continent. The United States was still at war with its former mother country England, in what later became known as the war of 1812.

It was in this time of world conflict and historical change that an expedition was organized and not so secretly supported by the United States to seize control of Texas from Spain. The Gutiérrez-Magee expedition known as the Republican Army of the North was led by Jose Bernardo Gutierrez de Lara and Augustus William Magee.[40]

One of the colorful personalities in the Republican Army of the North was Captain Josiah Taylor. He was one of several captains commanding the American units. He was born in Virginia in 1791. He got married in Georgia. He then left his wife and two young children temporarily to find adventure and treasure in Spanish Texas.

He and his men had good horses and were proven marksmen. In at least two of the battles with the Spanish Royalists, Captain Taylor's unit would be in the center of the line bearing the brunt of the attacks.

On August 7, 1812 they invaded Spanish Texas from the neutral territory of Louisiana proudly waving an "Emerald Green Flag" which was their war banner. The expedition quickly captured Nacogdoches, Trinidad de Salcedo and La Bahía (Goliad) where Magee died. After the capture of San Antonio, a Declaration of Independence for the first Republic of Texas was proclaimed on April 6, 1813. Unfortunately ... this independence was very short lived.

In response to the declaration of independence, a Spanish Royalist Army of more than 1,800 men was organized under commandant-General Arredondo. They marched in early August from Laredo toward San Antonio to put down the rebellion.

Toledo became the new commander of the Republican forces after deposing Gutierrez. The Republicans with a force of former royalists, Tejanos, Anglos and Indians set out to meet the Spanish army south of the San Antonio, to spare the city the destruction of war.

On August 18th the Republican rebels fell into a trap and were ambushed in a dense oak forest 20 miles south of San Antonio between the Atascosa and Medina Rivers. Under a blazing hot Texas sun, the Republicans began their battle already tired, thirsty, hungry and debilitated by the high humidity.

The intense battle involved artillery, cavalry, infantry and lasting four-hours before the Republicans broke ranks and ran. The battleground flowed with the blood of the Republicans. The vast majority of them not killed on the battlefield were captured and executed during the retreat.

The few survivors, such as Captain Josiah Taylor, rode at a full gallop towards the Louisiana border and safety. His life was spared by a combination of factors; a fast horse, luck and a high resistance to pain and trauma. How many of us could survive a trek of over 450 miles on horseback ... after receiving seven wounds in the battle, including two rifle slugs in your body?

Upon arriving in Louisiana the rifle slugs were removed. After a long recovery, Josiah returned to Georgia to his wife and two children. This would not be the last Texas would see of Josiah Taylor and his off-spring.

It was a disaster in that less than 100 out of a force of about 1400 survived the slaughter, while the Spanish forces lost only fifty-five men. These fifty-five were given an honorable burial on the march to San Antonio. The Spanish forces declared martial law and delivered brutal punishment to the rebels, their supporters and family members in San Antonio.[41]

The bodies of the fallen Republicans lost in the battle were ordered by the Spanish authorities to be left to rot under the blazing Texas sun. It wasn't until nine years later in 1822, when Jose Felix Trespalacios, the first Governor of Mexican Texas gave these skeletons and bones a Christian burial.

One of Spanish General Arredondo's subordinates was a Lt. Antonio López de Santa Anna. Santa Ana would return to San Antonio twenty-three years later in the Battle of the Alamo demonstrating some of the brutal techniques learned during the Battle of Medina.[42]

Although the Battle of Medina is virtually unknown to most Americans and Texans, it was the bloodiest battle ever fought on Texas soil. According to Historian Robert Thonhoff "More men died at the Battle of Medina than at the battles of the Alamo, Goliad and San Jacinto combined," Amazingly, the exact location of this historic battle is still unknown. (In 2008 the author and his sons Brian and Brandon Harrin participated in an unsuccessful expedition to locate the actual Battle of Medina site.)

Chapter 7: The Anglo Invasion

The Anglo invasion began first with the encouragement of the Spanish and later the Mexican governments. In 1820 Moses Austin a 59-year old Missourian asked the Spanish government for a large land grant that he proposed to promote and sell to American settlers.[43]

Based on Austin's background as a Missouri banker, Louisiana judge, Virginia mine operator and Philadelphia dry goods merchant, his request must have seemed outrageous.[44] However, the Spanish government had three problems it needed to solve: It needed a buffer against illegal Anglo settlers and it had a shortage of native Mexican settlers. Only 3,500 had settled in Texas (part of the Mexican State Coahuila y Tejas) and finally Spain needed to pacify or exterminate the more violent Indian tribes.[45]

In 1821 Mexico, of which Texas was a part, finally won its independence from Spain. Texas developed quickly under Mexican rule as the government promoted settlement by working with groups such as Austin's. Returning from a trip to Mexico City, Moses Austin died from exposure and exhaustion. His son Stephen took over and by the end of 1824 the colony had attracted over 250 colonists to Texas.[46]

Working with the Mexican government, Austin set up a sales organization of land agents. These land agents (Called empresarios) received 67,000 acres of land for every 200 families they brought to Texas.

The sales organization was wildly successful in spite of the Mexican government strict requirements for land ownership (1) Settlers must become Mexican citizens and (2) Settlers must be or must convert to Roman Catholicism. In spite of these restrictions, by 1830 there were 16,000 Americans in Texas. Although the Anglos weren't the majority in the State of Coahuila de Tejas, they made up a 4-to-1 majority in the northern (Texas) portion of the State.

The third goal of elimination of the more violent Indian tribes did not occur until around 1875 when the last of the original Indian groups of Texas had been killed or forced onto reservations in Oklahoma.

As the Anglo population exploded, the Mexican authorities became quite alarmed, not only by their numbers but by their actions. It was more than the exploding Anglo population that caused concern, it was also their actions. The Anglos segregated themselves from the native Mexicans, attended their own schools, refused to learn Spanish and primarily traded with the United States. Mexican authorities strongly suspected that the Anglos were a Trojan horse and these colonists would be used as a revolutionary force to annex Texas to the United States.

As a form of self-defense, Mexican authorities began a major crackdown. This included restricting trade with the United States, setting up new military posts, reaffirming their prohibition on slavery and ending Anglo immigration. [47]

By 1832 General Antonio Lopez de Santa Ana, became the president of Mexico and to the dismay of the American colonists, in 1834 Santa Ana made himself dictator of Mexico. When Stephen Austin went to Mexico City to negotiate with Santa Ana he was imprisoned for a year.

One of the key figures in the unfolding drama was Sam Houston. Houston was quite a character and ultimately instrumental in winning independence for Texas. At the age of 15 he ran away from home and lived with the Cherokee Indians in Southern Tennessee. He fought in the war of 1812, battled the Creek Indians under Andrew Jackson and at 30 served as a Congressman. At the age of 34 he was elected governor of Tennessee.

He was considered by many Americans as a future Andrew Jackson, until a scandal struck in 1829. Houston had married a woman 17 years younger than he was. Within just a few months the marriage was annulled, causing great embarrassment and humiliation. He became a drunkard and returned to live with the Cherokee Indians in what is now Oklahoma and Arkansas. Houston arranged peace treaties with enemy tribes and interceded on behalf of the Cherokee tribe with President Jackson demanding that the U.S. live up to its treaty. Jackson disagreed and instead sent Houston to Texas to monitor the American settlers and the growing anti-Mexican sentiment.[48]

In November of 1835 the American colonists created a constitution, and organized a temporary government without declaring independence from Mexico. While still hoping for self government through compromise, they created a protective military force with Sam Houston as commander.[49]

By the middle of 1835 scattered violence against Mexican rule began to spread until the entire Texas army of 300-500 riflemen captured Mexican military headquarters in San Antonio. This was the beginning of the revolution against Mexican rule.

Chapter 8: The Battle of the Alamo

The Texas revolution and the Battle of The Alamo were outgrowths of the Mexican civil war and Santa Ana's seizure of power in Mexico. Santa Ana was fighting a two front war.[50] He was fighting dissidents and consolidating his power within Mexico itself, while he began his campaign to liquidate Anglo infected rebels in Texas

The real revolution began on October 2, 1835[51] when Anglo settlers in Gonzales stopped Mexican troops from taking a small cannon that had been given to the town to protect against marauding Indians. This emboldened the revolutionaries who rapidly attacked and captured Mexican strongholds at Goliad and Lipantitlan.

By late October, the revolutionaries organized the Army of the People and marched to San Antonio de Béxar (San Antonio). They won some victories outside of the town, but were reluctant to assault Bexar. Although there were desertions of some settlers these seemed to be replaced by arriving volunteers from the United States by way of New Orleans. This changed on December 5th when the rebels captured San Antonio after a five-day battle.[52]

The Mexican garrison was allowed to leave Texas after they pledged not to return to reinstitute Mexican control.

Between December 1835 and February 1836 the sense of unity that had previously existed dissolved as in fighting intensified over what actions should be taken next. There were several schools of thought, regarding what needed to be done. The first; the fight had been won over Mexican authorities and the battle was now over. The second; Mexican troops would try to retake Texas in the spring. The third; the fight should be taken into Mexico itself, with the city of Matamoros and its custom house on the Rio Grande being the starting point.

After the Mexican troops were forced out of San Antonio de Bexar the rebel government ordered that a garrison remain in the town. Unfortunately two hundred of the garrison was rapidly stripped off for the Matamoros expedition, greatly weakening the ability of the rebels to defend Bexar, should Mexican troops return.

When General Antonio López de Santa Ana returned to Texas with a large column of Mexican troops, he found the rebel forces divided and unprepared. Santa Ana's objective was to reassert control over Texas.

To accomplish this he needed to capture the politically important center of San Antonio de Bexar (San Antonio) and then to put the entire rebel garrison to the sword as an example to any other rebels.[53]

A second military column, commanded by General José Urrea first marched to secure the city of Matamoros from the rebel threat. Upon securing the city, they marched to meet the rebels gathered around Goliad.

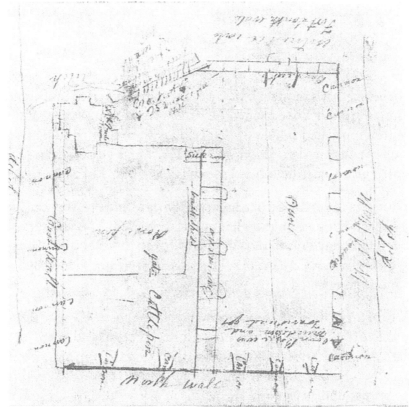

Figure 4 Alamo pen sketch before the battle of 1836 by Dr. John Sutherland

The Mexican forces reached San Antonio de Bexar on February 23 and began a siege of the Texian forces garrisoned at the Alamo Mission. The battle of the Alamo which was the most famous battle of the Texas Revolution began with the siege of the Texian rebels garrisoned at the Alamo Mission and ended on March 6, 1836.[54]

It was in the early morning of March 6 when the Mexican army launched their final assault on the Alamo. Although the small force of rebel Texians repulsed two attacks they were overwhelmed by the third and final Attack.[55]

The majority of the Texian rebels retreated into the long barracks (chapel). The rebels unable to get to the chapel tried to escape, but were slaughtered by the waiting Mexican Cavalry. The fighting was hand –

to-hand and room-to-room until Mexican troops controlled the entire Alamo.[56]

It is believed that a number of the Texans may have tried to surrender, but they were quickly executed on orders from Santa Ana. After the battle, the mutilated bodies of the Texians were burned in a pile and their charred bones left on the ground for over a year. General Santa Ana used techniques he learned so well at the Battle of Medina.

Eyewitnesses claim the Texian losses at 185 dead and the Mexican losses at 1544 dead with an unknown amount wounded. The few survivors included Colonel Travis' slave Joe, a Mexican deserter and primarily family members of the Texian soldiers. They were questioned by Santa Ana and then released.

As part of a psychological warfare campaign, Santa Ana sent three of the survivors to the rebel town of Gonzales to spread word of the Texian defeat. After hearing this news, the Texian commander ordered a retreat of the government and all the citizens towards the United States border and away from the Mexican army.[57]

Santa Ana grew furious after learning that his men had captured Colonel Fannin and his 350 rebel troops on the 20th of March and held them prisoner in Goliad. Santa Ana sent a courier on the old Ox-Cart Road through the future Helena to order the execution of Fannin and his men.

Santa Ana's orders were followed on Palm Sunday, the 27th of March.[58] The prisoners were divided into three groups, marched onto open fields, and shot.

All of Fannin's command except a few who escaped or were spared by the Mexicans, were slaughtered, their bodies stacked and burned.

Only three weeks after the massacre of the defenders of the Alamo, the victims of Goliad now served as martyrs for the Texians. A sense of total terror swept across what remained of Houston's forces and the vast majority of Texian civilians. They fled for their lives, in what has been called the "Runaway Scrape," towards the safety of the United States border to the East.[59]

It was only three weeks later, on April 21, 1836 that the Texians got their revenge. Driven with fury and inspired by cries of "Remember Goliad" and "Remember the Alamo," the outnumbered Texans in a dramatic reversal, won one of history's most decisive victories at the Battle of San Jacinto near present day Houston.[60]

Sam Houston and his rag tag band of 910 pioneers routed Santa Ana, the self-styled "Napoleon of the West." Approximately 700 Mexican soldiers were killed and 730 captured, while only nine Texans died ... amazingly, the battle lasted only 18 minutes.[61] Santa Ana was captured and forced to order his troops out of Texas, ending Mexican control of the area and changing the map of North America forever.

Chapter 9: Texas Is Now Free...But Not Free Of Trouble

After the Texian victory at San Jacinto the United States government decided to assess the situation in Texas. In the summer of 1836, United States President, Andrew Jackson, sent a State Department clerk, Henry M. Morfit, as a special agent to Texas. His task was to collect information on the republic's population, strength and ability to maintain independence.

Morfit filed his report in August 1836. His report estimated the population at 30,000 Anglo-Americans, 3,478 Tejanos, 14,200 Indians, of which 8,000 belonged to the so-called civilized tribes that had migrated from the United States. In addition he estimated a slave population of 5,000 plus a few free Negroes.[62]

Shortly thereafter, in the fall of 1836 Sam Houston was inaugurated as president of the independent country known as the Republic of Texas. The Republic of Texas claimed all of the present State of Texas as well as parts of present-day New Mexico, Oklahoma, Kansas, Colorado and Wyoming based upon the Treaties of Velasco between the newly created Texas Republic and Mexico.[63]

Although many Texians favored a rapid annexation by the United States, the U.S. Government did not favor annexation. Some of the reasons for this decision were: the unstable financial situation in Texas and the constant threat of war with Mexico.[64]

Although the battle of San Jacinto had been a decisive victory for Texans, Mexico continued to raid the Texas border, refusing to recognize Texas's independence. The new government of Texas was essentially bankrupt and had little governmental infrastructure in place.

After being rejected by the United States, the Texians began creating a government and an independent nation from scratch. Thousands of settlers continued pouring across the Texas border every year, in spite of continued fighting with both Mexico and hostile Indian tribes.

One of the major disputes between Texas and Mexico was related to borders. This was especially true with the southern border. Mexico insisted the border was the Nueces River, while Texas claimed it to be the Rio Grande River. Many threats and incursions came from both sides over this and other issues.

In 1841 Santa Ana again became president of Mexico and renewed hostilities with Texas. These hostilities increased after several invasions of Texas by the Mexican military. One of these was a raid by General Rafael Vasquez with 700 soldiers and their two day occupation of San Antonio. This raid set off a wave of fear and terror for Texians called the "Runaway of 42."

This was followed in September of 1842 by an attack on San Antonio by Mexican General Adrian Woll who dragged merchants and lawyers from their homes and businesses. These civilian prisoners were then sent on a forced march into Mexico. Upon reaching Mexico they were incarcerated at the infamous Perore Prison where they encountered physical abuse, humiliation and starvation.

By this time, sympathy for the Texian cause had grown rapidly in the United States and in early 1845 annexation was at last approved. Hostilities with Mexico and the Indians reached a settlement, and Texas was admitted as a state on December 29, 1845 ... after almost ten years as an independent nation.

To complicate matters the Mexican government on June 4, 1845 restated their old claim to Texas, eventually leading to war with the United States in 1846. Even before formal annexation General Zachary Taylor had been dispatched to Texas and by October of 1845 he had 3,500 troops on the Nueces River in order to repel a new Mexican invasion. After an attack on American forces, the United States declared war on Mexico on May 11, 1846.[65]

The full reality of the war with Mexico hit the Texas coast at Matagorda Bay like a hurricane on August 1, 1846. Throughout the day, army transport ships poured into the bay and anchored just offshore.[66]

This operation was commanded by the third highest ranking officer in the United States Army, John Ellis Wool. The sixty-two year old general exploded with nervous energy, as he came ashore to arrange for this massive landing. General Wool had served in the War of 1812, the current War with Mexico and would ultimately serve as a Union general during the Civil War.[67]

Wool sent thousands of troops and tons of military supplies in endless wagon trains up the Ox-Cart road from Lavaca (now Port Lavaca) to San Antonio for the ultimate invasion of Mexico. He chose to disembark at Lavaca because of the squalid, unhealthy conditions he found at the German immigrants' camp at the Port of Indianola.[68]

The old road went through Victoria on the 140 mile march to San Antonio. The heavy military wagons traveling this primitive road first encountered swampland up from the coast. From Victoria to Goliad was at first muddy after heavy rains, then sandy, and finally deep in dust up to San Antonio, through present day Karnes County.[69]

Although the road followed some of the original trails used by ancient Indian tribes and Spanish Conquistadores, it was totally inadequate to handle the heavy military traffic. The poor quality of the roads, shortage of building materials for repairs, and the scorching Texas sun made life difficult for both the soldiers and the civilian teamsters. Marching under the August sun between the groups of wagons, the foot soldiers were tormented by thirst.[70]

One of the early descriptions of the road between Matagorda Bay and San Antonio was made in August of 1846 by Lieutenant W. B. Franklin, topographical engineer under General Wool. He described the road from La Vaca through Goliad and Alamita (Future Helena) to San Antonio as follows: "Because the flies were so numerous the horse were nearly frantic and the men as well. For their comfort they had to travel at night." [71]

General Wool brought in his old friend Captain Robert E. Lee as an Engineering officer. Lee was charged with improving the South Texas roads to support a sustained invasion of Mexico. As part of this effort, Lee made numerous trips between the gulf coast and San Antonio including through the future Helena. This is the same Robert E. Lee who changed American history as the commander of the Confederate Army of Northern Virginia during the American Civil War.[72]

By the last week of September, Wool had transported over 1100 loads of supplies and at least 2,400 men to San Antonio. Doubling the population of the little city and putting a sharp strain on all its resources.[73]

The War between the United States and Mexico began with an attack on American troops by Mexican forces along the southern border of Texas on April 25, 1846. This bitter and brutal war ended when U.S. Gen. Winfield Scott occupied Mexico City on September 14, 1847; a few months later, a peace treaty was signed (February 2, 1848) at Guadalupe Hidalgo.

Under the terms of this treaty the United States acquired the northern half of Mexico. This area later became the U.S. states of California, Nevada, Arizona, New Mexico and Utah.

In return the U.S. agreed to pay $15 million to Mexico as compensation for the seized territory. Although the Mexican military leadership, tactics and weaponry was often lacking, the United States victory came at a very heavy cost, due to the bravery and tenacity of the individual Mexican soldiers.

The war cost the United States over $100 million, and ended the lives of 13,780 U.S. military personnel. In addition to the tremendous loss of territory, Mexican casualties have been estimated at 25,000 soldiers. Relations between the United States and Mexico remained tense for many decades to come, with several military encounters along the border.

U.S. General Zachary "Old Rough and Ready" Taylor's status as a war hero helped him capture the Presidency in 1848. In a strange twist of fate, President Polk, a Democrat, had pushed for the war that led to Zachary Taylor, a Whig, winning the White House.

During the war, hundreds of teamsters and trail drivers came to Texas, and were hired by the United States Army. They were the key to hauling the thousands of pounds of military equipment and food across Texas necessary to support the war effort.[74]

Once the war ended, many of the teamsters found work on the newly enhanced road system between the Gulf of Mexico and San Antonio, hauling both commercial and military supplies for the frontier forts.

A number of the more adventurous ones settled in the wild and still dangerous territories in what would become Karnes County and Helena. Some of the original settlers in this virgin territory were men like the pioneer H.H. Brockman, Trail Drivers Frank Wishert and Levi Watts.

These earliest of pioneers in South Texas and the future Karnes County faced many deprivations and dangers that could strike at any moment. In these earliest of days it wasn't just the desperados that could reduce your life expectancy, it was also hostile Indians.

As evidence, here is a newspaper article from Karnes County. Texas - NEWS - The Kenedy Times Historical Edition-October 31, 1963 about an Indian attack in the future Karnes County:

One of the first memorable dates in the history of Karnes County, Texas was Oct 8, 1848, at which time a fight with Indians occurred just above the junction of the dry Escondido Creek, three miles from Kenedy and about two and a half miles south of old Daileyville, in the Plez Butler pasture. A band of Indians, about forty in number, raided the Yorktown settlement and drove off some thirty head of horses, and a company of thirty white men headed by Capt. (John) York organized as quickly as possible and followed their trail to Escondido Creek. Here they discovered a blanket, supposed to have been left by the Indians, and as they stopped to examine it, a volley of shots was fired from a thicket nearby, and a fierce battle ensued. After about thirty minutes the York party had lost three men, including Capt. York, his son in law, James Beil, and a man named Sykes---and it was forced to withdraw because the Indians were hidden behind a large fallen oak in the dense thicket of trees, and greatly outnumbered the white men.

The news of the fight spread quickly to Goliad County where Jackson and Benson Burris organized a company of men who came to the scene of the battle and buried the three men who had fallen in battle. It is estimated by the Goliad party that seven Indians were killed and their bodies carried away.

Although this was one of the last major battles with Native Americans in the area, the dangers were far from over.

Chapter 10: Helena and Karnes County Begin

In 1852, San Antonio was little more than a village, and the surrounding country a wilderness, infested with wild beasts and wild men. On the very edge of civilization two men had a dream. Thomas Ruckman and Lewis S. Owings founded Helena at the site of a sleepy Mexican trading post called Alamita, in what was then considered Western Texas.

Alamita or "Little Cottonwood" was a tiny Mexican settlement founded in the 1840s. It was described as a little spring in a clump of cottonwood trees a few miles south of the intersection of Cibolo Creek with the San Antonio River.[75]

This settlement, in what later became Karnes County, was Located on a bend of the San Antonio River at the intersection of the Chihuahua Trail and the wagon road from Gonzales to San Patricio.[76]

The Chihuahua Trail or Ox-Cart Trail was first known as the la Bahia Road. The La Bahia Road was a major trade route connecting coastal Texas with Mexico and points west used to transport soldiers, settlers, supplies and treasure. This road ran from San Antonio to La Bahía (now Goliad) and the Texas coast.

Thomas Ruckman was originally from Pennsylvania and a graduate of what later became Princeton University. This adventurous young man of twenty-two, found his way to San Antonio, Texas on Christmas Day of 1850. Ruckman worked as bookkeeper for several firms in San Antonio until he made a fateful trip in 1852. He came through old Alamita by accident while traveling to Goliad in 1852. Here is his personal account of that trip which changed his life and that of his descendents;[77]

"In the summer of 1852 on my way back from San Antonio to Goliad, I found a little store and blacksmith shop on the road about ten miles after I crossed the Cibolo. This little storehouse was mostly built of rough boards that had been split in the woods out of post oak trees.

The proprietor... had a little while before that time purchased of Antonio Navarra agent Ramon Musquez a two hundred acre tract out of his four league grant (1 League = 4428.4 acres),[78] for which he paid one dollar per acre. On this tract where the cart road from San Antonio to the Gulf crossed it, he built his store, home dwelling and shop. Soon afterwards we laid out the town ... and named it Helena.

It is a beautiful location. A mile from the river on dry elevated ground - soil partly sand so that it is never muddy about the streets, always dry underfoot... And no place in the state surpasses it for health. Eighty-five miles in a straight line from the bay, the Gulf breeze strikes it fresh."

Ruckman had stumbled across a very unique location at Alamita. Much of early Texas history had traveled this ancient highway.

The old Ox-Cart road had witnessed: Native American hunter-gatherers, Spanish conquistadores, priests, heroes of the Alamo, Santa Ana's messenger ordering the death of Fannin's 300+ men in Goliad, Polish and German settlers, Robert E. Lee, followed by Confederate and Union cavalry, and of course the ever present outlaws and desperados ... followed by quick shooting lawmen.

The transport of freight on the old Ox-Cart road utilized a variety of methods. This included overloaded pack animals, ox-carts with two huge wheels, prairie schooners, and Wells-Fargo type wagons drawn by sixteen mules. By the late 1840s, stagecoach service started on the Ox-Cart Road, with the only stop between Goliad and San Antonio being the halfway station of Alamita.[79]

Alamita was quickly renamed in honor of Dr. Owings's wife, Helen, as both men enthusiastically entered into a business partnership. They envisioned a substantial city at this important road stop. Ruckman built a gristmill and formed a partnership with Owings to open a general store.[80]

Ruckman and Owings hired Charles A. Russell, the Goliad County Surveyor to survey and plat the new site and the town was officially established as a town November 7, 1853. That same day, a post office was established and Ruckman served as first postmaster.

The population around Helena increased so rapidly that the partners initiated a campaign to create a new county from parts of Bexar, Gonzales, DeWitt, Goliad and San Patricio counties.

Through their efforts the state legislature created Karnes County on February 4, 1854, named in honor of the late Texas revolutionary hero, Henry Wax Karnes, with Helena as the County seat. Here is the reason Lewis Owings chose the name Karnes for the new County.

Henry Wax Karnes, a native of Tennessee, was sixteen when his family moved to Arkansas. One of his friends and neighbors there was Lewis Owings. In 1835 Karnes came to Texas and was serving as an overseer on Jared Groce's Bernardo plantation on the Bravos River when the Texas Revolution began. His heroic exploits in Texas inspired his old friend Dr Owings to suggest in 1854 that this new county be named after Karnes.[81]

The first election of county officials was held February 27 on the porch of the Ruckman-Owings store, which provided papers, pens, ink and the tables used by the voters.[82]

It appears that at this point in time Helena already had over 200 residents and there were over 200 voters in this election. Naturally, women and children were not counted in this county vote so the population was considerably higher than this vote count for the county.[83]

A two-story courthouse was built at Helena in 1856 from frame clapboard construction. The first floor served as a courtroom and for church services as well as Saturday night dances. The upper level was used as a Masonic lodge room for the Alamita Lodge No. 200. [84]

The original wooden courthouse was destroyed by a tornado during the civil war in 1863. It wasn't until 1873 that a two-story stone courthouse replaced the original building. (That two-story stone courthouse is still standing today).

In 1854 not long after the founding of Helena there was a large immigration from upper Prussian Silesia. The immigrants had been abused by the Prussians (Germans) for centuries, starved and treated like Serfs. These Poles with Father Leopold Moczygemba, founded Panna Maria near Cibolo Creek, not far from Helena, It is the oldest Polish colony in North America and as you will see shortly, they had a tremendous influence on Karnes County and Texas.[85]

Chapter 11: The Early Years in Helena

Although the town of Helena and the Karnes County were growing by leaps and bounds not everyone was benefiting from this growth. The pioneer founders clearly were having serious "cash flow" problems with their general store as indicated by the following notice in a San Antonio newspaper.

NOTICE

ALL PERSONS INDEBTED TO THE

undersigned are respectfully informed that they

will do well to call and settle, or their accounts will be

left in the hands of a proper officer for collection, as

we are very much in need of money.

Our terms hereafter are

NO CREDIT --- Goods Cheap for Cash.

DEER SKINS, BEEF HIDES AND PECANS

WANTED!!

OWINGS & RUCKMAN

Helena, Texas, Nov. 9th, 1854   4-1y

Figure 5 Western Texan San Antonio, Nov. 25, 1854

That same day, Owings and Ruckman advertised in the Western Texan newspaper their new line of fall and winter goods had just arrived from New York and Boston. Naturally, everything must be paid for in cash.

```
┌─────────────────────────────────────────────────────────┐
│                      NEW GOODS!!                          │
│                                                           │
│                  OWINGS AND RUCKMAN                        │
│                                                           │
│              Helena, Karnes County, Texas                 │
│                                                           │
│         OWINGS AND RUCKMAN respectfully                   │
│         inform the citizens of Karnes County, and of      │
│         Western Texas generally, that they are now receiving │
│                                                           │
│                  FALL AND WINTER GOODS                     │
│                                                           │
│         carefully selected in New York and Boston for this │
│         Market consisting of a large and full assortment of │
│                                                           │
│         FANCY and STAPLE DRY GOODS, READY MADE             │
│         CLOTHING, BOOTS, SHOES, HATS,                      │
│         CAPS, &c. &c. HARDWARE and CUT-                    │
│         LERY, TINWARE, and STONEWARE                       │
│                                                           │
│         CROCKERY and GLASSWARE,                            │
│         STATIONARY AND PERFUMERY,                          │
│         FAMILY GROCERIES,                                  │
│         Nails, Rope, Bruches (sic), Steel corn and        │
│         Coffee Mills, Rifles, Shot Guns and Pis-          │
│         tols, Oils and Paints, Umbrellas, Carpet          │
│         and Travelling Bags, Clocks, Violins and          │
│                                                           │
│         YANKEE NOTIONS,                                    │
│                                                           │
│           Also a large and general assortment of          │
│         Drugs and Medicines                               │
│         Together with all of DR. JANES Patent Medicines,  │
│         &c., &c., &c.                                      │
│                                                           │
│           All of which we will sell low for cash; we have │
│         but one price, and no goods to leave the store unless │
│         PAID FOR, so that we are able to sell at reduced  │
│         rates.                    The Western Texan        │
│                                   San Antonio, Nov. 25, 1854 │
└─────────────────────────────────────────────────────────┘
```

Much of the history of South and Central Texas took place along the roads that radiated from San Antonio in every direction. During the stagecoach era of 1847 through 1881 over fifty different stage lines operated in and out of San Antonio.[86]

At this time, San Antonio and the future Helena were at the very western edge of the Texas frontier and highly vulnerable to the dangers of a land with little law and order. A toxic combination of outlaws, marauding bands of Indians, Mexican soldiers and banditos made both travel and commerce life threatening pursuits. This was especially true

48

before the Mexican War of 1848, as pointed out in a Houston newspaper article in 1845, which stated in part:

"The trade of Bexar, like that of Corpus Christi, has been completely broken up by the Comanche who have driven back or cut off every party of traders that were accustomed to visit those places."[87]

The first bridge across the San Antonio River at Helena seems to have been initiated by Owings as you can see in the following State of Texas document:

An Act to authorize L.S Owings and his Associates or Assigns to make and maintain a Toll Bridge across the San Antonio River. L.S Owings and his associates or assigns and their successors, be authorized to make and maintain a bridge across the San Antonio River, opposite the town of Helena in Karnes County, suitable for the passage of wagons, carriages, etc and after completion of the same the proprietors shall be entitled to demand and receive the following rates of toll, for each road wagon, one dollar, for each cart, fifty cents, for each carriage or other light vehicle, fifty cents, for each animal and rider, ten cents, for each footman, five cents, for each single horse, mule, or other animal, five cents, for each animal (other than horses) in a drove, two cents. That no person shall be allowed to construct any other bridge across the said river within ten miles of the bridge hereby authorized, for five years after it's construction. That said L.S Owings and his associates shall have the work completed in five years from the date of this charter, or they forfeit all rights to the same. Passed, September 1ˢᵗ 1856. (The Laws of Texas 1822-1909 Volume 4 1898 by H.P.N Gammel)

Apparently it was not until 1854 that a straight-line stagecoach route was available from Indianola to San Antonio. This straight-line route seems to have followed the old Ox-Cart road from the old La Bahia on the Texas coast to San Antonio. Previously the stagecoach routes tended to take a much longer through population centers such as New Braunfels, Seguin, Gonzales, and Victoria.

The advertisement below from late 1854 offers a new line of Four Horse Coaches from San Antonio to Victoria *via* Helena and Goliad. It was started by L.S. Owings the partner of Thomas Ruckman of Helena. Helena had just become the county seat of the newly formed Karnes County. As Helena was located almost midway between Goliad and San Antonio along the old Ox-Cart Road, it was destined to become a boom town for decades to come.

Figure 6 San Antonio Western Texan November 23, 1854

Initially Owings stagecoach line ran weekly from San Antonio to Victoria via Helena and Goliad. However according to the advertisement, stages were scheduled to run twice a week after September 1, 1854. Owings resided in Helena for only a few years, when he left suddenly to become the first territorial governor of Arizona.

As you can observe in these original newspaper advertisements from 1854 and 1856 Helena's commercial activities were expanding at a rapid pace ... way before the American Civil War.

Figure 7 Upper advertisements from Lavaca Herald September 13, 1856, lower advertisement from Western Texan April 11, 1854

Unlike Lewis Owings, Thomas Ruckman had fallen in love with Helena and was laying down his permanent roots in his town. Shortly after marrying Miss Jeanie Long, Ruckman met an itinerant brick maker from Kentucky in the spring of 1856. The brick maker determined that the soil on the banks of the San Antonio River would make high quality bricks based on the correct proportion of sand to clay.

The two men came to the following arrangement:

Ruckman would build a kiln and a hand mill along the river, while the brick maker would provide the building materials for Ruckman's new home.

Ruckman's new galleried, two-story, brick and cottonwood home built along the San Antonio River in 1857 required about 90,000 of these new bricks. Ruckman's double-walled house was a copy of Ashley Hall at Princeton University.

Figure 8. Thomas Ruckman house-Courtesy of the Karnes County Museum, Helena, TX

Ruckman was a natural entrepreneur. Within six months, he created a work force of twenty Polanders (Poles), hired from nearby Panna Maria and they turned out some 300,000 bricks from the Ruckman kiln.

Ruckman also built a large gristmill for mealing corn. He quickly determined that the cost of pine lumber imported from Florida was impeding the growth of Helena. To solve this problem Ruckman built a sawmill along the San Antonio River, using sawed lumber cut from native trees along the river. This dramatically lowered building costs as his local lumber was much cheaper than the imported Florida pine.[88]

Ruckman's new businesses provided most of the brick and lumber used to build most of the stores, homes, ranches, and fences in early Helena.

Thomas Ruckman enlarged his general store as ranchers and farmers in the area became regular customers. Ruckman was involved in every aspect of Helena's rapid growth. In addition to being its founder, he was a prominent merchant, banker, Postmaster and later became both the principal and a teacher at the Helena Academy.[89]

Ruckman invited his younger brother John, and his three sisters, Rachel, Rebecca, and Lizzie, to move from Pennsylvania to live with him. His younger brother, John, moved to Karnes County in 1857, and rapidly became a prominent citizen, merchant, rancher, farmer, banker and eventually Postmaster.[90]

Well, we have talked quite a bit about the men of South Texas. However, what was life like for the average young woman ... before the Civil War and the women's liberation movement? Here is a fascinating view of the kind of advice provided to "Well-bred" women in those early times in South Texas? This is an actual advice column for woman from the Indianola Texas Courier newspaper in 1859.

INDIANOLA [TX] COURIER, July 30, 1859, p. 4, c. 1
Plain Hints on Personal Behavior.—A well-bred lady is always known by her perfect ease and tranquility of her manners. These points are to be carefully cultivated. Acquire, if possible, an easy confidence in speaking, so as never to appear abashed or confused, taking care, however, not to fall into the opposite error of forwardness or presumption. Persons moving in the highest circles of society, seldom, or never allow themselves to appear disturbed or vexed, whatever occurs to annoy them. Perhaps there may be an affectation of indifference in this; still, their conduct is worth admiring, for everything like fidgetiness or boisterousness of manner is disagreeable to all who witness it.

Everything like the following will, of course, be carefully avoided by a real lady, in her personal behavior. Loose and harsh speaking; making noises in eating or drinking; leaning awkwardly when sitting;

rattling with knives and forks at the table; starting up suddenly, and going unceremoniously out of the room; tossing anything from you with affected contempt or indifference; taking anything without thanking the giver; standing in the way when there is merely room to pass; going before any one who is looking at a picture or any other object; pushing against any one without asking pardon for the unintentional rudeness; taking possession of a seat in a coach, or place of public meeting, which you are informed belongs to another; intruding your opinions where they are not wanted, or where they would offence [sic]; leaving acquaintances in the street, or a private company, without bidding them good-bye, or at least making a bow to express a kindly farewell; slapping any one familiarly on the arm; interrupting any one in conversation with you; telling long and tiresome stories; whispering in company; making remarks on the dress of those about you, or upon things in the room; flatly contradicting any one instead of saying, 'I rather think it is otherwise,' 'I am afraid you are mistaken,' &c.; acquiring a habit of saying, 'says she,' 'says he,' 'you know,' 'you understand,' &c.

Here is another opportunity for you to actually picture what lifestyles were really like and what people actually thought and felt in early Helena. This is an actual interview with one of the very early inhabitants of old Helena, Lyman Russell son of Charles A. Russell the first Karnes County surveyor, provided the following testament:

"The town of Helena was laid off in 1852 by 'Doc' Owings as to the southwest part, and Elyah Spencer for the northwest part." The new town was in Goliad County and Charles A. Russell, my father, county surveyor of that county did the surveying and plotting. The town was called Helena after Mrs. Owings whose name was Helen. We moved to the new town in January, 1853 and first lived in a log house. Later we built a homestead of sawed oak with a cotton wood floor, all from the Ruckman sawmill.

Owings and Ruckman were associated together in the mercantile business in an original building of adobe facing on the public square where later the courthouse was built. This was on Goliad Street.

Helena was on the main traveled road between old Goliad and San Antonio, the famous old Mexican "Cart Trail. Doc Owings left Karnes County in 1858 to take the governorship of Arizona under appointment of President Buchanan.

Other pioneers I recall were Odell who kept an adobe tavern, and had a big sign, : The Traveller's Home." It was swinging out over the Goliad road just where you cross the little bridge now out from Helena going to Runge.

There was Thomas Ruckman a Princeton Graduate, and my earliest ideal of all that a man should be; a gray old Frenchman whom we children called "Uncle Mishy"; Gordon Case the first man to make sorghum molasses in Karnes County; Helena's mayor, C.C. Cotton, who was father of Mrs. Al Mayfield and of Mrs. Lockhart; N. Hess Jones, a lawyer from Gonzales who was the first head of the Helena Massonic Lodge, Oliva Reed Smith, the blacksmith, also the town fiddler for dances.

Jim Garner who when only fifteen years of age killed W.H. Bateman on Christmas Eve 1856; Charles Talor who killed Yach Polk and among many others William Dial, a Texas Ranger who when we moved to Helena, had two big turkeys hung up outside the door, and had a big new coffee boiler, and a tin bucket both full of honey inside for us.[91]

Chapter 12: The Cortina Wars

Juan Cortina was one of the most dangerous men in South Texas and the Mexican border region. He had a significant impact on Texas history affecting its citizens including those in Helena and Karnes County. To Mexicans on both sides of the border he was a combination Tejano Robin Hood and a symbol of military resistance to Anglo racism. To the Anglos in Texas he was a dangerous killer and a savage animal.

Cortina was born in Mexico just south of the Rio Grande River to a wealthy cattle ranching family. Sometime in the 1840's he moved north of the Rio Grande into territory claimed by both Mexico and Texas.[92]

During the Mexican war he served as part of an irregular cavalry unit during the battles of Resaca de la Palma and Palo Alto under General Mariano Arista of the Tamaulipas Brigade. After the war he returned to the north bank of river where he was indicted twice by a Cameron County grand jury for stealing cattle. Cortina had little fear of going in public as his political influence among Mexicans insured he would not be arrested. [93]

By the late 1850's after the United States had annexed all lands north of the Rio Grande, Cortina had become an important political boss for the South Texas Democratic Party. Although the United States had invalidated many of his land claims, he still remained a large rancher. Cortina hated an elite group of Anglo judges and attorneys in Brownsville. He accused them of stealing land from Mexican Texans using the American judicial system ... to make it legal. He became a hero and leader to many of the poorer Mexicans who lived along the banks of the river.

The event that radicalized Juan Cortina took place on July 13, 1859 in Brownsville, Texas. It began when he witnessed an Anglo city marshal pistol-whipping one of his former family employees. Outraged,

Cortina demanded that the marshal stop beating the Mexican and when the marshal refused, Cortina shot him in the shoulder, took his former servant up onto his horse and fled with him to safety.[94] With this classic blow struck for Mexicans, the Cortina legend and his career as an outlaw had begun.

Figure 9 Juan Cortina-Courtesy Library of Congress Washington D.C.

Just two months later, on September 28 Cortina led an armed force back into Brownsville. After taking control of the city he released Mexicans whom he felt had been unfairly imprisoned and executed four Anglos who had killed Mexicans, but hadn't been punished.

Cortina proclaimed the Republic of the Rio Grande as his followers raised the Mexican flag and shouted, "Death to the gringos!" But

Cortina did not pillage or terrorize the city. Instead, he soon withdrew to a nearby ranch where he issued a proclamation invoking the "sacred right of self-preservation" and condemning the fact that so many were "prosecut[ed] and rob[bed] for no other cause than that of being of Mexican origin."[95]

The six months following the Brownsville raid were called "Cortina's War." The Texas Rangers struck back furiously, often indiscriminately punishing any Hispanic in the south Rio Grande Valley. Cortina, who soon had five or six hundred armed men under his command, resumed his raids when the Rangers executed one of his lieutenants in Brownsville. The Mexican government, fearing that Cortina's actions would embroil them in another war with the United States, sent a joint Mexican-Anglo force against Cortina, which he quickly defeated.

Here is a sensationalized newspaper article showing the depth of anguish and concern in the Anglo community of Texas. Pay particular attention to one of the participants, Karnes County Sheriff John Littleton from Helena, as you will be seeing him again soon.

THE RANCHERO [Corpus Christi, TX], December 3, 1859, p. 2, c. 2 from our Extra of the 30ᵗʰ.

Cortina Still Triumphant!
Four Americans Murdered, and
their Bodies Mutilated.
Latest from Brownsville!!

Corpus Christi, Texas, Nov. 30, '59.
Mr. Mat Nolan, Sheriff of Nueces county, has just arrived from Brownsville, this Wednesday evening, 30ᵗʰ of November, having left that city on Sunday last at noon.

He reports, that on Sunday, the 20ᵗʰ of November, a detachment of 30 men of Tobin's command had a fight with a part of Cortina's men on *the Palo Alto Prairie, where McCay, Dr. Mallett, Greer of San Anto-nio, and Fox of Live Oak, were killed, <u>Lieut. Littleton, Sheriff of Karnes county, severely, though not mortally wounded</u>, and several other men more or less slightly wounded.*

On Monday, the 21ˢᵗ November, he (Mr. Nolan) assisted at the burial of the slain Americans, and found their bodies dismembered in a most disgusting and horrible manner.

On Tuesday, the 22d November, under command of Capt. Tobin, 200 volunteers sallied out from Brownsville in search of Cortina. Their advance guard of some 20 men, under command of Lieut. Pugh, came on the enemy, about nine miles from Brownsville, at about noon, and found them in position, strongly entrenched and fortified. From their fortifications a most galling fire of round shot, grape and canister was opened upon the advance party, and an overwhelming force of the enemy at the same time approaching them on the flanks, they were driven in, and falling back upon the main body of Americans, hotly pressed by Cortina and his followers, retreat became general.
On Wednesday, the 23d of Nov., Capt. Tobin with 250 men, dis-mounted, and having with them a 24 Pound Howitzer, again sallied out to attack Cortina at his fortified camp, but after a careful recon-noissance of the approaches and position, it was deemed necessary to withdraw without making the contemplated attack.

Fifty Regular U. S. Troops were in the Barracks at Brownsville, but did not join the volunteers or participate in any of the skirmishes.

Six American prisoners, in the hands of Cortina, at the time of the hanging of Cabrara, had been killed in "retaliation."
The Mexican flag is flying above Cortina's fortress. His scouts were seen at various places as far out as 45 miles from the city of Browns-ville.

The forces or strength of Cortina have not been overestimated, nor the condition of affairs in Brownsville, or the hardships undergone by hits inhabitants since Sept. last, been exaggerated or overrated.

Some wealthy and connected Mexican residents of Texas opposed Cortina and quietly aided his opponents. However the bulk of the Tejano population supported him, often sending his troops supplies and refusing to help U.S. officials. But this support proved to be no match for the U.S. Army which dealt Cortina a sharp defeat in Rio Grande City on December 27, 1859.[96]

Sporadic raiding and fighting continued for several months. Observers reported settlements deserted, property destroyed and normal business activities cancelled along the 100-mile stretch of the border from Brownsville to Rio Grande City.

Forced to dissolve his army and retreat to Mexico, Cortina continued his military activities there, fighting with Benito Juarez and other Mexican nationalists against French intervention in the 1860s and aiding Union partisans in Texas during the American Civil War. In 1863 he was made a general in the Mexican Army and later became the acting governor of Tamaupilas. In 1876 Mexican dictator Porfirio Diaz imprisoned Cortina in Mexico City where he was held until 1890. He died in Tamaupilas in 1892.[97]

Chapter 13: The First Outlaws

Living on the edge of civilization your personal security and the protection of your livestock and property was primarily in your hands. At that time frontier justice in Karnes County was quick and summary. For example, it is reported that late one evening five men charged with horse- stealing were placed in jail. The next morning when the sheriff arrived ... they were found hanging from the limbs of the two live oak trees outside the jail. A man might get away with murder in Helena or Karnes County but he better not try horse stealing.[98]

Violence was a way of life in old Helena and the toxic combination of alcohol and a dispute could have a fatal result for one or both of its participants. Below you will find an old newspaper article of one such example in old Helena.

THE RANCHERO [Corpus Christi, TX], August 11, 1860, p. 2, c. 4

Melancholy Affair.—We regret to learn that a serious affray occurred on Wednesday, at Helena, Karnes county, between <u>*Capt. John Littleton and John Rabb.*</u> *According to our information Rabb fired the first shot from behind Littleton, striking him on the side, the ball striking the temple, and glancing, scalped the forehead which stunned him so that he did not repeat his fire. Littleton fired two more shots—the first passed through the cheeks, and the last through the body of his antagonist. Littleton's shots having been expended, it is said some unknown person fired at Rabb, the ball striking him in the body. Strange to say, Rabb did not fall, and was still alive when our informant left Helena, though in a very precarious condition. Capt. Littleton, though very seriously wounded, was not considered in any great danger.*
The difficulty, it is supposed, grew out of an old feud.—Goliad Messenger.

Things were always tough and dangerous in Helena, especially for its lawmen. Even in the time of the earliest Karnes County Sheriff's, such as S. Boutwel, there were revealing comments made about the sheriff's job "which from all reports was a position that required either a man of Viking boldness or one of suicidal tendencies, for it is said that few, if any, in these wild days, ever survived his term of office."[99]

Clearly, as the troubles increased Helena needed a way to restrain the bad guys. The first jail in town was a wooden structure in the northwest corner of courthouse square.[100] It apparently lacked bars and cells. Locals recalled that the sheriff would take his prisoner to a blacksmith shop, fit him with shackles, than chain the jailbird to some immovable object within the building.

In addition to random violence, there was always the possibility of running into one of the many outlaws and desperados in Helena and South Texas that could reduce your lifespan in the blink of an eye.

One of the most colorful outlaws and desperados to ever ride through Helena, South Texas and the old west between the 1840's through the 1860's was feared by men, women and even children.

This legendary figure in Texas history spoke Spanish like a native, was an expert roper, horse trader, freighter, Indian fighter, a first class cusser and a lover. Surprisingly, the name of this feared, desperado was Sally Skull.

Sally Skull was a dead shot with a pair of cap-and-ball pistols that were strapped to her waist. She rode with and bossed a tough gang of Mexican vaqueros (cowboys), roped and rode as well as any man. She could pick flowers with her black snake whip or leave a scar on any man who crossed her. She could out shoot most men with her rifle and kept her bowie knife sharp and ready.

Sally Skull was born in the Illinois Territory in 1817, and christened as Sarah Jane Newman. She was the fifth of ten children born to Rachel and Joseph Newman. Her grandfather William Rabb had fought in the war of 1812 against the Indians.

In 1822 her parents and grandfather, William Rabb, were among the first Anglo settlers of Stephen F. Austin's "Old Three Hundred" in Austin's colony. This was the Texas equivalent of the Pilgrims arriving at Plymouth Rock.

Her Grandfather William Rabb received the largest grant in the colony in return for agreeing to build a gristmill and sawmill on the Colorado River. The family's land grant of over 22,000 acres included the present site of La Grange in Fayette County.

Unfortunately for the Rabb clan their land grant was at the northern most portion of the Austin Colony and Indians were a constant danger. The Indians would continually steal their horses, shoot though the cracks of the log cabin if the oil lamps were left on and attack the log cabins, if the men folk were gone at night.

At a very early age Sally understood about the dangers of the wild-west and learned to be as self reliant as the bravest of men. One night when the men folk were gone, one of the marauding Indian braves noticed the door of the log cabin did not touch the ground. He put his feet under the door in order to lift it off its hinges so he could break in and claim his prize. Unfortunately for him, Sally's mother Rachel surgically removed his toes with a quick slash of her double edged sharpened ax. The Indians then tried to enter the home by way of the chimney. A feisty Rachel piled feather pillows in the fire grate and set them ablaze ... causing great discomfort to the home invaders.

In those primitive frontier times, before there was an ACLU or a local police department, survival was a more useful tool than a formal education. Sally learned how to survive, ride and shoot as good as any man ... if not better.

Due to the continuous attacks by the Indians as well as the theft of horses and corn, the family had to relocate to a more secure location. In 1824 the entire family moved down the Colorado River to a more settled area, upriver from present day Wharton where Joseph Newman and two of the Rabb sons obtained titles to their grants.

Her father died in 1831 and not long after she married the first of her five husbands. Her first husband was Jesse Robinson who in 1823 had joined a company of volunteers, predecessors of the Texas Rangers. Sally probably first met him when she was a young girl of seven. Jesse and several other men had rescued the family when about 180 Waco and Tawakoni Indians had attacked their house.

Jesse continued soldiering after their marriage and fought in the Texas Revolution. He became an elite trooper for Sam Houston in the battle of San Jacinto and according to legend fired the shot killing the cannoneer in the center of Santa Ana's main line.

As both Sally and Jesse were confrontational and had warrior personalities, the inevitable divorce came in 1843. She claimed cruel treatment and Jesse claimed abandonment and charged her with adultery.

She married George H. Scull 11 days after her divorce. She kept his name for the rest of her life, except she preferred the spelling of Skull.

She lived in Dewitt County in 1850 but in 1852 she moved to Banquete in Nueces County and set up a permanent ranch there. She attended Henry Kinney's great fair at Corpus Christi that year when the famous military hero and Indian fighter John S. "Rip" Ford wrote his memoirs years later he recalled seeing her in action. While riding home from the fair, he heard the report of a pistol, raised his eyes, saw a man falling to the ground and a woman not far from him in the act of lowering a six-shooter. She, a noted character, named Sally Skull. She was famed as a rough fighter. Prudent men did not willingly provoke her in a row. It was understood that she was justifiable in what she did on this occasion having acted in self defense. [101]

In the mid-1850s a European tourist recorded her activities and reputation. "The conversation of these bravos drew my attention to a female character of the Texas frontier life, and on inquiry. I heard the following particulars. They were speaking of a North American Amazon, a perfect female desperado, who from inclination has chosen for her residence the wild border-country on the Rio Grande.

She can handle a revolver and a bowie knife like the most reckless and skillful man: she appears at dances (fandangos) thus armed, and has even shot several men at merry-makings. She carries on the trade of cattle-dealer and common carrier. She drives wild horses from the prairie to market, and takes her oxen wagon along through the ill-reputed country between Corpus Christi and the Rio Grande." [102]

Sally didn't need the excuse of self-defense to start shooting. She has been described as "a merciless killer when aroused" and apparently it didn't take much to get her aroused.

She had gained a reputation of making snap decisions as to who needed killing and then quickly following through for some unfortunate victim. Sally was also known to have a strange sense of humor.

On one occasion Sally was told a stranger had been bad mouthing her behind her back. She tracked down the alleged perpetrator and quickly confronted him and saying loudly "So you been talkin' about me? Well dance you son of a bitch!" Sally then pulled out her six shooters and began rapidly firing at his quick-moving boots that had begun a very fast dance routine in the dusty South Texas street. [103] No one today knows what the original remark was that got Sally so upset. It must have been a real beauty.

On another occasion Sally crossed paths with a freighter who owed her money. She is said to have grabbed a large ax and said loudly, "If you don't pay me right now you son-of-a-bitch, I'll chop the goddam front wheels off every Goddam wagon you've got." The freighter made a quick decision, paid his debt to Sally ... and, according to legend lived to tell the tale. [104]

Sally was known to be fearless and in the 1850s began making danger-ous trips across the border into Mexico for horses. Either with her vaqueros or alone she carried large amounts of gold. She reputedly only had a problem once during a solo trip through the territory of Juan Cortina. Cortina the very dangerous bandit and leader of hundreds of bad men with a savage reputation jailed her for a few days. Reputedly,

Sally considered it as a kind of a vacation and just relaxed while waiting for her Mexican vaqueros to arrive.

Her reputation was so wide spread that back in the day in Texas, if a child was still frisky after dark, momma simply said; If you don't go to sleep, Sally Skull is gonna cum and get ya. This usually achieved the desired result as the rambunctious children jumped into bed ... and quickly pulled the cover over their head.

When the Civil War began Sally seized an opportunity to make a lot of money quickly. Texas cotton was in great demand by European manufacturers, but the north had a naval blockade of Texas and Confederate ports. Likewise Texas and the Confederacy desperately needed military supplies and equipment. Since international law forbade the Union blockaders from interfering with Mexican commerce, Sally dropped her horse trading and became a major transporter for the confederacy. [105]

Sally and her Mexican vaqueros turned teamsters moved huge quantities of Texas cotton to European ships loaded at Matamoros on the Mexican side of the Rio Grande. The sale of Texas cotton provided the money for the large scale purchase of military supplies shipped into Mexico from Europe and then transported to the Confederate forces.

Sally and her men became a regular fixture on the famous Cotton Road. This Cotton Road was the major route to transport contraband goods to and from the neutral port of Matamoros, Mexico. Much of the Confederate cotton bound for Mexican ports was routed through Helena, and it also became a receiving facility for clothing, medicines, smuggled food, arms, and ammunition. [106]

Starting from Matamoros, Mexico through South Texas, Helena, Goliad and to the railroad at Alleyton (near present day Columbus) Confederate cotton went south and European weapons were shipped throughout the Confederacy by rail from Houston by way of Alleyton. [107]

By the end of the Civil War, Sally Skull became quite wealthy having acquired an abundance of gold. She had married her fifth and final husband Christoph Horsdorff around 1860 when she was in her early 40's and he was in his early 20's. Everyone called him "Horsetrough" because they claimed "He wasn't much good, mostly just stood around." Legends abound that soon after the war Horsetrough ambushed and killed her for her gold and then buried her in a shallow grave. Whatever the truth of her ultimate demise, Sally Skull was one of the most unusual characters in the history of the old Southwest.

Chapter 14: The Ox-Cart War

Hidden under the blacktop of Farm Road 81 in today's Helena, lays an ancient superhighway used centuries ago by buffalo and Indians, During Spanish colonial times this superhighway was first known as the La Bahía Road and later the Ox-Cart Trail or Ox Cart Road.

This old Ox-Cart Road has always been critical in the history of Karnes County. This road carried substantial commercial activity between Chihuahua, El Paso, and New Mexico via San Antonio. The total trade was considerable amounting to millions of dollars per year.

Helena, being at a mid-way point between San Antonio and Goliad, served as a rest stop for cart drivers to eat, drink, and relax. By the time Helena was founded in 1852 the old Ox-Cart Road was bursting with traffic. According to the memoirs of Thomas Ruckman:

"The large amount of freight may be understood when we realize that not only the settlers, but also all of the various posts of the American Army, strung for many hundreds of miles along this frontier that reaches from the Rio Grande to the Indian territory, must be supplied in this round about way.

As there is such a vast amount of goods to be hauled we can see it kept not by the tread of feet. There are some two thousand carts owned and driven by Mexicans and drawn by three or four yoke of oxen. There are also Mexican mule trains made up of great lumbering wagons, each with from ten to twelve mules in front of it. Besides these there are the clumsy American wagons hitched to five or six yoke of the biggest and longest horned oxen in the world.

All of these slow moving vehicles, constantly crawling one after another in a steady stream, remind me of a great cloud of smoke that seems to be winding and worming its way along the road. Day after day, month after month, year after year, this great serpent keeps crawling on over the hills and prairies' past our town, along the river's edge, and onward, to finally disgorge itself in that coming city that lies to the north and west of us, San Antonio.[108]

By the late 1850s traffic on the Ox-Cart Road had increased dramatically for the transport of goods between San Antonio and Indianola (Powderhorn) on the Gulf Coast. The trouble began in 1857 after San Antonio merchants tired of paying exorbitant fees of $3.00 per hundred pounds [109] to American drivers hauling freight to and from Indianola.

In order to drive these prices down hundreds of Mexican drivers and their carts were imported because they would haul freight cheaper and work for lower wages than the Americans.

The Mexican drivers quickly gained a virtual monopoly on the Ox-Cart Road due to lower pricing. The American drivers became resentful and tensions increased dramatically between these competing drivers.

Adding to the problem were accusations and resentment against the Mexicans by Texas slaveholders and cattlemen. Slaveholders claimed the Mexican teamsters had helped runaway slaves escape to Mexico. The Texas cattlemen were also incensed that the Mexican drivers were stealing, butchering and eating their cattle grazing along the Ox-Cart Road.

This resentment exploded into violence around Helena in 1857 as the so-called Cart War began.

First it started as low level sabotage by jobless Texas freighters. They would sneak into the Mexican camps at night and cut the spokes of the cart wheels. Naturally this caused the wheels to collapse at the first turn the next morning. Unfortunately, such low-level sabotage quickly escalated into full scale guerrilla warfare near Helena and Goliad as Texans destroyed the Mexican's carts and stole their freight. [110]

The shootouts and bloodshed increased leading to significant injuries, deaths and loss of revenue. Local and county authorities seemed either unable or unwilling to stamp out the escalating violence.

The San Antonio merchants demanded the protection of soldiers for their Mexican cart drivers. After significant political pressure was applied General D. E. Twiggs, the General of the Department of Texas, began providing military escorts.

The protection provided to the Mexican drivers by the Army was insufficient to stop the attacks as emotions built to a fever pitch in both Bexar (San Antonio) and Karnes Counties.

What began as a war of words began to escalate quickly. A mob from San Antonio led by a Colonel Wilcox came down to Cibolo Creek in Karnes County, bragging they were going to burn down the town of Helena. While camped on the creek (their bravery disappearing like their supply of whiskey) they came across four or five innocent local citizens and threatened to hang them. A vote to hang the locals was defeated by a small majority. The mob then denounced the citizens of Karnes County as murderers and thieves.[111]

December 4, 1857 a public meeting at Helena passed eight resolutions. In Number Six, the citizens of Karnes County resolved that the continued presence of "peon Mexican teamsters" on the Ox-Cart Road was an "intolerable nuisance" and requested that the citizens of San Antonio withdraw them and substitute other drivers. [112]

As the deaths and injuries increased, commerce was disrupted and the road became unsafe for everyone. Texas Governor E.M. Pease was forced to send in the Texas Rangers and by early 1858 the war was over. [113]

The Ox-Cart war left a bad taste in the mouth of many in South Texas. As a result, Mexican drivers realized that cart driving was not worth the risk to life and limb and headed back to Mexico. American teamsters became a familiar sight on the cart road, until they too were displaced after the railroad came through Karnes County in 1886 and the Ox-Cart Road finally was abandoned.

Chapter 15: Knights of the Golden Circle

Figure 10 an original K.G.C. symbol from 1861

The Knights of The Golden Circle or KGC has been called "The Most Gigantic Treasonable Conspiracy the World Has Ever Known."[114] This secretive and dangerous organization was the catalyst for the American Civil War. It ripped the country apart and left wounds that still bleed to this day.

The true role of this secret organization, also known as The Sons of Liberty or the American Knights was one of the best kept secrets of the Civil War. After the Confederate surrender the KGC secretly planned a second Civil War, and its remnants may still be active to this day. Our modern "politically correct" history books have for some reason chosen to ignore this truth.

Many years before the Civil War the KGC had planned a slave empire called the Golden Circle to be centered in Havana, Cuba. This empire would include the southern portion of the United States, Mexico, Central America, the Caribbean and the northern part of South America. [115]

The leadership of the KGC claimed that their empire would have a virtual monopoly on key raw materials such as tobacco, sugar and cotton. This virtual monopoly would give them the economic power and muscle to maintain and expand the system of slavery.

It has been claimed that the KGC was intimately involved with the secession of the Confederate States, a planned invasion of Mexico, the opening salvos of the war at Fort Sumter, South Carolina, Guerrilla attacks in the North and the Border States and the assassination of President Abraham Lincoln.[116]

It is also believed that many of the post Civil War attacks on northern bank and railroad interests by outlaws such as Jesse James and post war terrorism against African Americans by the KKK are directly related to the Knights of the Golden Circle.

One of the founders of the KGC was George W. L. Bickley[117] a Virginia-born doctor, editor, and adventurer. The records of the KGC convention in 1860 indicated that the organization originated in Lexington, Kentucky on July 4, 1854; However the KGC did not become active until 1859 when Bickley undertook an organizing campaign across the southern states.

Bickley called for the annexation of Mexico, which proved popular in Texas. Within a short period of time Bickley had organized thirty-two "castles" or local chapters in various Texas cities, including Houston, Galveston, Austin, San Antonio, Helena, Marshall, Jefferson, and La Grange.

Although many prominent Texans joined the K.G.C., one that got away was Governor Sam Houston. Although Houston was for the annexation of Mexico, he would not join nor would he support the KGC because of its anti-Union position. Ultimately he was forced to resign as governor because of his refusal to support Texas secession.[118]

Today, we have no understanding of the depth of anger and fear that was felt by day to day Southerners before and after the election of Abraham Lincoln. Below are samples of the news the people of South Texas and Helena were reading at that time. Naturally, the combination of these news stories and the election of Lincoln were like throwing gasoline on a fire. Membership of the KGC exploded as the prominent citizens of towns like Helena joined the KGC.

BELLVILLE [TX] COUNTRYMAN, August 4, 1860, p. 2, c. 6

The Abolition Plot in Texas.

We extract the following from a letter to the Houston Telegraph, from Dallas, giving further particulars of the extensive Abolition plot discovered there a few days ago:
The outhouses, granaries, oats and grain of Mr. Crill Miller, were destroyed a few days after the destruction of Dallas. This led to the arrest of some white men, whose innocence, however, was proved beyond a doubt. Several Negroes belonging to Mr. Miller, were taken up and examined, and developments of the most startling character elicited. A plot to destroy the country was revealed, and every circumstance even to the minutiae, detailed. Nearly or quite a hundred Negroes have been arrested, and upon a close examination, separate and apart from each other, they deposed to the existence of a plot or conspiracy to lay waste the country by fire and assassination—to impoverish the land by the destruction of the provisions, arms and ammunition, and then when in a state of helplessness, a general revolt of the Negroes was to begin on the first Monday in August, the day of election for the State officers. This conspiracy is aided and abetted by abolition emissaries from the North, and by those in our midst.
The details of the plot and its modus operandi, are these: each county in Northern Texas has a supervisor in the person of a white man, whose name is not given; each county is laid off into districts under the sub-agents of this villain, who control the action of the Negroes in the districts, by whom the firing was to be done. Many of our most prominent citizens were singled out for assassination whenever they made their escape from their burning homes. Negroes never before suspected, are implicated, and the insurrectionary movement is widespread to an extent truly alarming. In some places the plan was conceived in every form shocking to the mind, and frightful in its results. Poisoning was to be added, the old females to be slaughtered along with the men, and the young and handsome women to be

parceled out amongst these infamous scoundrels. They had even gone so far as to designate their choice, and certain ladies had already been selected as the victims of those misguided monsters.

Fortunately, the country has been saved from the accomplishment of these horrors; but then, a fearful duty remains for us. The Negroes have been incited to these infernal proceedings by abolitionists, and the emissaries of certain preachers who were expelled from this county last year. Their agents have been busy amongst us, and many of them have been in our midst. Some of them have been identified, but have fled from the country; others still remain, to receive a fearful accountability from an outraged and infuriated people. Nearly a hundred Negroes have testified that a large reinforcement of abolitionists are expected on the first of August, and these to be aided by recruits from the Indian tribes, while the Rangers are several hundred miles to the North of us. It was desired to destroy Dallas, in order that the arms and ammunition of the artillery company might share the same fate.

Our jail is filled with the villains, many of whom will be hung and that very soon. A man was found hung at our neighboring city of Fort Worth, two days ago, believed to be one of those scoundrels who are engaged in this work. We learn that he had stored away a number of rifles, and the day after he was hung a load of six-shooters passed on to him, but were intercepted. He was betrayed by one of the gang, and hence his plans were thwarted. Many others will share his fate.

I have never witnessed such times. We are most profoundly excited. We go armed day and night, and know not what we shall be called upon to do.

In order to educate you further on what really was in people's minds, I offer this newspaper letter to the Editor in the Port of Indianola. Remember this was only days before the dreaded election of Abraham Lincoln to the presidency ... a southern nightmare to be sure.

INDIANOLA [TX] COURIER, October 27, 1860, p. 2, c. 3 Correspondence of the Crisis.]

Anti-Wide Awakes.

Saluria, Texas, Oct. 10, 1860.

Messrs. Editors:--Feeling a deep and abiding interest in the wellbeing of the South and its institutions, and the perpetuity of the Union—hallowed by so many glorious achievements—founded upon integrity, honor, and a just regard to the equality and rights of the several States constituting it, and the feelings and prosperity of their citizens; entertaining an abhorrence of the rapine, murder, insurrection, pollution and incendiarism which have been plotted by the deluded and vicious of the North, against the chastity, laws and prosperity of innocent and unoffending citizens of the South; and regarding with irrepressible indignation and contempt, a threat conveyed in a speech recently delivered by W. H. Seward, of N. Y., in which he exults in the early advent of the "irrepressible conflict," (of which he is the arch instigator,) which he declares to be already on hand; congratulates the "Wide-Awakes" upon their timely organization, and exhorts them to maintain it until after the election; and believing that Lincoln is the chosen champion for this conflict and this organized Northern canaille for "repressing" and degrading the South; the undersigned respectfully submits to his fellow-citizens of Texas, the following propositions, commending them to the true men of the North and South.

1ˢᵗ. That in the event of Lincoln's election as President of the United States, in November next, the undersigned will contribute one thousand dollars towards arming and equipping the first company of anti-Wide Awakes, of one hundred men, that may be raised, officered and uniformed, in the State of Texas.

2d. That he will give said company, or any other of like character that may be raised in Texas, one hundred dollars each, not exceeding ten in number, who may expel from this State any appointees, who may accept office under Lincoln. Believing them to be the most dangerous enemies to the peace, prosperity and continued Union of the States.

The above propositions are separate and distinct, and I ask you to retain this, my obligation, and deliver it to the company or companies entitled to its benefits and who claim its execution. To the fulfillment of which I hereby pledge my sacred honor; and solemnly appeal to my fellow citizens, whether the times do not call for action, not resolves, when four hundred thousand Northern bayonets are bristling, ready to be plunged into the best blood of the South?

Hugh W. Hawes.

The majority of Texans along with a majority of voters in 10 other slave states cast their Presidential vote for Southern Democrat John C. Breckinridge of Kentucky. As the results below clearly show, the slave states were on the losing end of the election and their worst nightmare became reality.

THE PRESIDENTIAL ELECTION OF 1860 [119]

Candidate	Party	Popular Vote	Elec. Vote	%Pop. Vote
Abraham Lincoln	Republican	1,865,593	180	40%
Stephen A. Douglas	Northern Democrats	1,382,713	12	30%
John Breckenridge	Southern Democrats	848,356	72	18%
John Bell	Constitutional Union	592,906	39	12%

In Texas and throughout the country, the Knights of the Golden Circle formed the heart of the secession military machine as the crisis of the Union deepened.

The KGC gathered troops at the Rio Grande on two occasions for a planned invasion of Mexico but these attempts bore no fruit. The KGC did have great success in the takeover of all Federal "Union" facilities in Texas virtually without a fight. On February 18, 1861 "Castles from many parts of Texas including Helena took part after forcing General David E. Twiggs to surrender all U.S. military posts in Texas, including the headquarters in San Antonio. [120]

Very few Americans today have ever heard of the KGC, This organization at one point is believed to have expanded to several hundred thousand members throughout the south, the west and to a lesser extent the north during the Civil War. They were organized into lodges called "castles," with Masonic signs, grips, and passwords.

As mentioned earlier very few accounts of the Civil War make any reference to the Knights of the Golden Circle nor its covert activities to terrorize and demoralize the north throughout the war.

The government of Abraham Lincoln was so concerned about the KGC that they infiltrated the organization. Felix Stidger was an undercover United States Government Secret Service Agent who infiltrated the KGC and rose to the level of Grand Secretary of State Order of Sons of Liberty, State of Kentucky, 1864.[121] His testimony was later used to convict members of the organization on charges of treason.

In the north and border-states there were thousands of supporters known as Copperheads. The North considered them like the poisonous snake. They were actually peace democrats seeking a peace treaty with the south while in many cases supporting the KGC goals. There were many secret missions by the KGC and Confederate secret service that wreaked much havoc in the north and may have extended the war by tying up significant numbers of Union troops.

Here are just a few of those missions and plots:

Little known today and rarely ever seen in any history of the Civil War, a bold plan formulated by a number of Southern "castles" with support from northern "castles" in Indiana, Ohio and New York. The plan was to assassinate Lincoln at his inauguration, seize Washington D.C., and loot the U.S. Treasury striking terror into the hearts of the Northern abolitionists "and thus secure the entire field in advance." [122]

"The plan called for about a thousand men armed with bowie knives and pistols to meet secretly in Baltimore where they were to secure the services of the Plug Uglies (a violent street gang and political club). Thence proceed to Washington on the day preceding the inauguration, and stop at hotels as private citizens, after which their leaders were to reconnoiter and select the most effective mode of operations for the succeeding day." The plot was discovered and General Scott had sufficient troops and artillery to remove the winds from the sails of the plotters.

A group of thirty Confederate raiders on 19 October 1864 attacked the town of St. Albans, Vermont. Although they succeeded in terrorizing the citizens and robbing the town's banks they failed in their objective of burning the town to the ground. Although some of the raiders were captured after returning to Canada the Canadians refused to extradite them back to the United States. [123]

Confederate agents tried "to set New York City aflame." On 25 November 1864 the plot was put together by Robert Martin. He and seven other Confederate agents, including his second-in-command John W. Headley, made their way from Canada to New York City. The saboteurs set fires to more than a dozen buildings but all of the fires were extinguished without major damage. The eight arsonists made their way back to safety in Canada. Later one of them, Robert Cobb Kennedy, was captured in Detroit, transported back to New York, tried and hanged. [124]

There was a variety of weapons and techniques used by the KGC and Confederate Secret Service agents and operatives to wreak havoc and cause terror in the north and the south. Here are a few actual devices used by agents meant to sap the will of the Union to continue the war. [125]

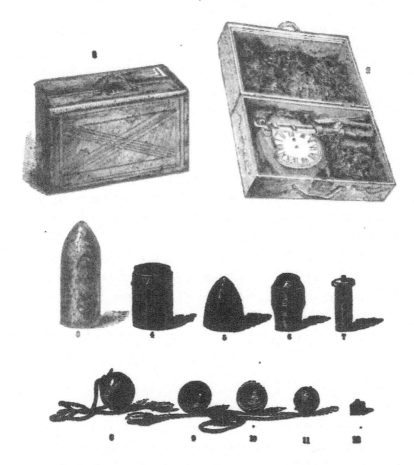

EXPLANATIONS of the INFERNAL MACHINES

Figure 1 A seemingly harmless portmanteau or hand valise. Figure 2 Shows the same opened, and its arrangement. An alarm clock with the bell removed, set to any given time, when running to that time springs the lock of the gun, the hammer of which striking and exploding a cap placed upon a tube filled with powder fires a train connected with a bottle of Greek Fire. The explosion of these combustibles ignites a bunch of tow saturated with turpentine with which the remainder of the valise is filled.

This innocent looking but vicious valise can be taken to ones room in a hotel, aboard a steamboat, or into a business house, or anywhere.

The clock wound up and alarm attachment set for any future time of from ten minutes to ten hours , the valise closed and locked, and at the time for which the alarm is set the slight explosion will occur without even attracting the attention of those nearby until the fire has been set and under full headway.

Figure 3 shows a conical shell 3 1/2inches in diameter and 8 inches long. Figures 4 and 5 show the bottom and top part of Figure 3 when unscrewed at the base of the cone: Figure 6 is a shorter shell into which Figure 7 is screwed, the space between figures 6 and 7 to be filled with the liquid Greek Fire: figure 7 is a case to contain powder, with a nipple for a cap at the upper end: figure 7 screws into figure 6 containing the Greek Fire, and the two forming an inner shell fitting loosely into figure 3, into which it is placed. When the figure 3 shell is discharged from a gun on striking any object the cap on figure 7 explodes and ignites and explodes the powder, bursting the shell and igniting the Greek Fire, and setting on fire anything with which it may come into contact.

Figure 8 shows a spherical shell or hand grenade ready for use: Figure 9 and 10 show the same shell or grenade unscrewed in the center for placing in it the interior shell: Figure 11 is a shell enough smaller than Figure 8 to admit the placing of nine nipples on the outside of it and have caps on each of them, and still work loosely enough that upon the shell or grenade dropping onto or striking anything one or more of the caps will explode: figure 12 is a small vial to contain Greek Fire.

The vial (figure 12) containing the Greek Fire is placed inside the smaller shell (figure 11) and the space between the vial and (figure 11) is filled with powder, and the two halves screwed together, and with the caps on the nipples figure 11 is placed in figure 8, which is then screwed together. The dropping of this shell or grenade eight or ten inches on the floor or any solid substance will invariably explode one or more of the caps, no matter which way it falls: or it can be thrown by hand, and on striking a building, or any object, one or more of the caps would explode, igniting the powder and bursting the shell, and the Greek Fire would set fire to a building or any other inflammable object with which it may come into contact. The string attached to figure 8 will enable a person to throw it a greater distance as a sling with less danger of its explosion in his own hand.

There have been a multitude of investigations alleging that many famed characters from the Civil War era, including John Wilkes Booth and Jesse James, belonged to and acted under the influence of the KGC. [126] A number of investigators argue that the KGC buried millions of dollars stolen from U.S. Army payrolls, banks, stage coaches and trains across the Southwest. Their claim is that this stolen money (now worth billions) continued to be guarded into the mid-twentieth century and maybe to this day. [127]

At this point you might be thinking what does all this have to do with Helena and Karnes County? Karnes County and the County seat of Helena became a hot bed of pro-secession activity ... well before the start of the Civil War. Some of the pro-secession attitudes can be attributed to radical anti-abolitionist newspapers. However, the major factor in radicalizing the County and creating a hatred for Abraham Lincoln and the north was the KGC.

The KGC had a major "castle" in Helena giving it significant "boots on the ground" in its campaign to gently nudge any Unionist's or wavering secessionist as to the error of their ways ... if you get my meaning.

Although there were about 32 KGC "castles" in the State of Texas by late 1860, as you can see from the following newspaper article the "Castle" at Helena appears to have been a prominent KGC center of power.

MEMPHIS DAILY APPEAL [MEMPHIS, TN], May 7, 1861, p. 2, c. 4

Knights of the Golden Circle.

Headquarters, Army of K. G. C., Louisville, Ky., May 1, 1861.

1. Commandants of K. G. C. castles throughout the various States of the South, excepting Texas, are hereby ordered to forward, without delay, to general headquarters, at Louisville, Ky., complete muster rolls of military companies. If the military organization of a castle is not completed, the commandant will take immediate steps to have it done. Each company, when organized, shall consist of one captain, one first lieutenant, two second lieutenants, four sergeants, four corporals, two musicians and ninety privates.
2. Castles belonging to the Texas division will report to Gen. Geo. W. Chilton, marshal of di[illegible]on, at Tyler, Smith county, Texas, or to Col. Charles A. Russell, acting adjutant general, at Helena, Karnes County, Texas. The president begs the order to respond fully and promptly to the call of Generals Chilton, Ford, Wilcox and Green, and stand on the defensive until our national troubles are ended.

3. All general, field and staff officers of the American legion will report immediately by letter or otherwise, to the president at Louisville, Ky.
4. The president begs to state for the information of the order that since the first of February last he has been laboring in Kentucky—principally in the city of Louisville—and has added to the order 1,483 members, 534 of whom have been sent to the army of the Confederate States. Two regiments are now being formed in the State to be held subject to the orders of the Governor. The order has now 17,643 men in the field, and the president has no hesitation in saying that the number can be duplicated if necessity requires.

George Bickley, K. G. C.,
President of American Legion.

Charles A. Russell the original Karnes County surveyor is shown as an acting adjutant general of the KGC. A number of other prominent citizens of Karnes County were both Mason's and members of the Helena "castle." One of the more well known members was John Littleton.

Littleton owned two slaves and had a background as Karnes County Sheriff, Texas Ranger, Indian fighter, veteran of the Cortina wars, Karnes County delegate to the Texas Secession Convention and later as heroic Confederate cavalry officer.

Although there were many prominent members of the KGC "castle" in Helena most of the membership records have either become unavailable or were destroyed to protect the guilty and occasionally the innocent.

Chapter 16: The Civil War

The American Civil War remains as the bloodiest war in American history. The war resulted in the deaths of 620,000 soldiers and an undetermined number of civilian casualties. Ten percent of all northern males 20–45 years of age died as did 30 percent of all southern white males aged 18–40. [128]

The Civil War tore the nation apart sometimes pitting brother against brother, family against family and neighbor against neighbor. Although this war ended almost 150 years ago it traumatized the entire nation and its effects can be felt to this day throughout the nation, Texas and certainly in Karnes County.

The seething anger of many African Americans and attitudes of some whites, are a direct result of the Civil War, the subsequent Reconstruction period and the racial angst that has festered like an open wound ever since.

As discussed in the years leading up to the Civil War, the United States was beset with conflict and controversy over the issues of slavery and states' rights. However nowhere in the south was the situation more complex than in Texas. Remember Texas had only been part of the United States for 15 years when the secessionists won their State wide election.

Although a good number of Texans supported the Union the political attacks on Southern institutions and the undercover activities of the KGC helped the secessionists win the vote. To demonstrate the effectiveness of the KGC in the vote to secede let's look at what happened in Karnes County. The final vote tally in Karnes County was 153 for secession and 1 against.[129] There is no record of who the 1 vote against secession was or how quickly his family collected on his life insurance policy ... if he had any.

Many Union sympathizers paid a huge price for not supporting the secession. As an example let's take the Singer family (as in sewing machines) who had a ranch on Padre Island before the war. Like many other Unionists they had to abandon their homes and leave. The rumor was that they had buried $80,000 in gold on their property but couldn't find it upon returning in 1867 due to hurricane damage. [130]

The federal arsenal at San Antonio was forced to surrender by the KGC and local militia on February 18, 1861 before the formal secession of Texas.[131] After the start of the war San Antonio served as a Confederate depot and several units such as John S. "RIP" Ford's Cavalry of the West were formed there.

The formal secession of Texas occurred on March 2, 1861 as Texas became the seventh state in the new Confederacy. In that same month, when Governor Sam Houston refused to declare loyalty to the Confederacy he was removed by the Texas secession representative John Littleton. [132]

In Texas this war began like most with great enthusiasm, patriotic fervor and overconfidence. By the end of 1861, more than 25,000 Texans had joined the Confederate army. During the war this number swelled to almost 90,000 Texans who served in the rebel army. They gallantly fought in every major battle of the war from New Mexico to Pennsylvania.

Unfortunately for the Confederacy and Texas, the deck was stacked against them as you can see for yourself in this very revealing chart.

RESOURCES OF THE UNION AND THE CONFEDERACY, 1861 [133]

	Union	Confederacy
Number of States	24	11
Population	23,000,000	8,700,000*
Real and Personal Property	$ 11,000,000,000	$ 5,370,000,000
Banking Capital	$ 330,000,000	$ 27,00,000
Capital Investment	$ 850,000,000	$ 95,000,000
Manufacturing Establishments	110,000	18,000
Value of Production (annual)	$ 1,500,000,000	$ 155,000,000
Industrial Workers	1,300,000	110,000
Railroad Mileage	22,000	9,000

*40% were slaves: 3,500,000

Just prior to the Civil War in 1860 Karnes County had a population of 2,170 with a fairly large foreign born population (primarily Polish) totaling 450 or 21% of the total population. This part of Texas was different than many other parts of Texas and the south in general. Rather than a typical southern plantation economy Karnes County was better suited to raising cattle. This probably accounts for the relatively small slave population of 327 or 15% of the total population. [134]

In spite of not being a plantation economy Karnes County residents voted overwhelmingly for secession as previously stated, 153 for to one against. This was apparently due to two factors: the high powered KGC "castle" in Helena and the fact that most Polish residents although opposed to slavery, could not vote because they had not resided in the state long enough to acquire citizenship.

At the start of the Civil War the majority of the county's residents actively supported the Confederate cause. Several companies of militia were organized in the county including the Escondido Rifles and the Helena Guards. The Helena Guards was a company of fifty-seven men organized on May 4, 1861 with Charles A. Russell elected as Captain, L.D. Cook, J. R. Cooke, and G.W. Brown, Lieutenants, John Ruckman as First Sergeant and Levi Watts as a Second Corporal. [135]

Each man was required to provide his own arms and equipment. The guards were among the units that participated in the Rio Grande campaign. Some of the Poles joined a unit known as the Panna Maria Grays. However generally, the Polish and German immigrants were not supportive of slavery or of the Confederacy. [136]

This anger and distrust of foreigners and pro-Union Texans became quite evident early in the war. In August 1862 many Germans were killed by Confederate forces in the Battle of Nueces as they tried to escape to Mexico and then to Union occupied New Orleans. In addition forty suspected Unionists were hanged in north Texas at Gainesville in October 1862. Two others were shot as they tried to escape. [137]

Naturally this lack of support for the Confederate cause led to great suspicion and animosity towards the foreign population. The Poles and other foreigners resented being forced to serve in the army and always tried to avoid Confederate officials. The relationship between the Poles and the Anglos continued to deteriorate when it was discovered a number of Poles had deserted to the north. One example is Peter Kiolbassa who joined the Confederate Panna Maria Grays as a bugler, but ended the war as a Captain in command of a company of the Union Army's 6th U.S. Colored Cavalry.

Quite a few of Karnes County's young men served honorably and with distinction during the Civil War. Captain John Littleton, Captain Thomas Raab Company A Frontier Regiment, LT. James P. King 3rd Frontier District TRT, Sergeant John Ruckman- Helena Guards, William G. Butler Private- Escondido Rifles, Monroe Choate raised the Escondido Rifles and served as its Captain. Captain Charles A. Russell and First Sergeant John Ruckman, Helena Guards 29th Brigade 24th Cavalry. Oliver Hazard Pearson Company I of the 2nd Texas Cavalry (AKA 2nd Texas Mounted Rifles). Those are but a few of the many men from the Helena area who served in the war.

In addition Helena's importance could be demonstrated by the fact that it was one of only seven towns in Texas with a Confederate Post Office authorized to print and issue its own stamps. [138] A single one of these original stamps could be worth upwards of $10,000 today. The postmaster in Helena from 1861-1863 was David W. Dailey. You will hear more about him later.

The fact that so many of its able-bodied men were serving in the army, caused an unanticipated problem for the citizens remaining in Karnes County. Deserters, desperados and all manner of bad guys took advantage of the relatively defenseless home front.

Karnes County became increasingly endangered by bands of Mexican renegades and bandits which, according to one group of Karnes County residents in late 1863, were "alarmingly on the increase and threaten to devastate the Country.[139] Unfortunately order could not be fully restored until the victorious Union Army established a military post in Helena long after the war ended.

Another major problem arose for all the citizens in Karnes County and throughout the Confederacy. Toward the end of the war the paper currency notes of the Confederacy became nearly worthless. A common story at the time was that a man could go to the market with a basket full of Confederate notes and come home with his meat in his little vest pocket. The notes were hardly acceptable anywhere, and transactions were done the old fashioned way, by barter and exchange.

Along with a worthless currency there were wartime shortages and inflation, [140] causing hardships for those who remained on the home front. Compounding these problems was a protracted period of drought lasting from 1862 to 1865.

The blockade of Texas by the Union Navy resulted in shortages of many basic commodities. Coffee, medicine, farm implements, paper, shoes and clothing were in short supply. Due to the lack of paper several Texas newspapers suspended or discontinued operations at various times and Governor Lubbock encouraged Texans to go back to their roots by making homespun clothing. Also during the war years,

Helena was called upon to provide several thousand bushels of corn for Confederate troops stationed along the Rio Grande.

However, Texas was better positioned than most Confederate States, due to its border with Mexico. Texas sent cotton to Mexico in exchange for military supplies, tobacco, medicines, dry goods, food, iron goods, liquor and coffee.

Large wagon loads of cotton passed through Helena and Karnes County to Matamoros, Mexico on the Rio Grande across from Brownsville and then to the Mexican seaport village of Bagdad. Here waited hundreds of ships from Europe and the United States taking advantage of this lucrative two way trade. As a result of this two way trade Helena and Karnes County residents were less affected by the shortages than most other areas of the Confederacy. However, as the war continued Texans were being devastated by the almost total loss of value of the Confederate currency and the huge price increases as demonstrated in the following commodities chart.

A COMPARATIVE COMMODITY PRICE INDEX IN TEXAS

Product	1861	1862	1863	1864
Butter	.25 ¢ lb	.27 ¢ lb	$1.75 lb	$9.00 lb
Salt	.06 lb	.06 lb	.15 lb	.28 lb
Bacon	.16 lb	.17 lb	.55 lb	1.75
Lard	.15 cwt	.18 cwt	.60 cwt	6.00 cwt
Corn	.67 bu	.70 bu	4.20 bu	25.00 bu
Flour	6.00 cwt	6.75 cwt	43.00 cwt	50.00 cwt
Wool	.15 lb	.27 lb	---------	---------
Tallow	.08 lb	.11 lb	.65 lb	13.50 lb
Beef	.02 lb	.06 lb	---------	.25 lb
Potatoes	1.75 bu	.60 bu	4.75 bu	20.00 lb
Meal	--------	.77 lb	4.75 lb	30.00 lb
Rice	.11 lb	---------	---------	6.00 lb
Coffee	.65 lb	---------	2.75 lb	30.00 lb
Molasses	.36 gal	---------	2.50 gal	25.00 gal
Sugar	.08 lb	.12 lb	.35 lb	7.00 lb

1861-1864

PRICE OF MILITARY STOCK IN TEXAS-1864

Artillery horse $400.00/head

Cavalry horse $325.00/head

Work oxen $125.00/yoke

SLAVE TRADE IN HOUSTON-1864

Ordinary negro man $4,500.00

Negro women l8-20 yr. . . . $4.000.00

Woman w/2 children. . . . , .$5,700.00

Young negro boy. $2,500.00

Young negro girl , ...$2,000.00

SOURCES: Houston "Tri Weekly Telegraph," Galveston "Tri Weekly News," Marshall "Texas Republican"

The Indian threat on the Texas frontier during the Civil War acceler- ated dramatically because of the shortage of manpower due to the war. Frontier troops did their best to keep the Indians in check with some success but couldn't stop them.

As an example a vicious raids by Kiowa and Comanche in the fall of 1864 left a dozen Texans dead and seven captured. The raid occurred along Elm Creek in Young County. Another problem for the frontier troops was they were given other duties in addition to the Indian threat. The frontier troops spent quite a bit of time arresting deserters, enforcing Confederate conscription laws, controlling Unionist activity and chasing outlaws and renegades.

Things were so bad that even men of marginal ages had to be called up for service or they volunteered. Here is an example: In February of

1864 the men of Captain Creed Taylor's company, a small group who had volunteered to serve in the Confederate "Provisional Army" began service. Taylor's twenty-five man troop was mustered in at Helena, Karnes County. [141] Remember Creed Taylor as you will be learning a lot more about him ... and his family.

As you can see by the following letter from Colonel RIP Ford more Helena men had to be called up by Confederate forces. One wonders if Captain Creed Taylor's unit fought as part of Colonel Ford's Confederate Expeditionary Force in the Rio Grande battles against the Union forces.

Although some historians have claimed that the Taylor's never fought for the Confederacy and that they only used pro-south rhetoric to cover their thievery and murder, it appears they may be incorrect regarding this fact.

HEADQUARTERS EXPEDITIONARY FORCES,

Camp near Banquete, March 22, 1864.

Capt. E. P. TURNER,

A. A. G., C. S. Army, Maj. Gen. Magnifier's Hdqrs.

B. : SIR: I have the honor to forward, for information of the major- general commanding, copy of communication from Colonel Bena- vides,* and also to report that I have sent couriers in every direction to hurry up the marching troops. I expect Colonel Showalter here within two days, also two companies from Helena, Captain Jones' company from Goliad, Captain Peflaloza's from San Antonio, making in all 1,000 men. With these I shall attack the enemy in the rear. I shall move up the Nueces, and prevent the enemy from making a dash upon San Antonio should he attempt it. I shall operate upon his rear, let him move as he may. The junction of Colonel Benavides and the troops at Eagle Pass will swell his force to some 500 men. The companies raised by Captain Fly, which are to organize on the 26th instant, and those of Colonel Sweet, if he has sent them forward, will augment my command to 2,000. With these I think I shall be able to defeat the enemy. We have two pieces here, .and I have ordered Captain Christmas to move others to the front as soon as he can. There is no grass in various portions of the country. Unless I can march from point to point where there is grass, tne country is absolutely impracticable. I regret that many of the men have no means to carry ammunition, except in haversacks or their pockets. I hope the major-general commanding will forward as many Enfield rifles as possible.

I have the honor to be, your very obedient servant,

JOHN S. FORD,

Colonel, Commanding

However by the spring of 1865 the situation was grim for the Confederacy. Mass depression swept over the Southern states with the news of Robert E. Lee's surrender at Appomattox.

After Texas units of the Army of Northern Virginia dropped their weapons everyone in Texas knew the end was near. In spite of the horrible news from Virginia, General E. Kirby Smith, Trans-Mississippi Department commander and General John Magruder, in charge of the Texas district, ordered in-state troops to remain at their posts. [142]

In early May Confederate units beginning in the eastern part of the state deserted en mass and began heading home. The civilian government also began to collapse quickly as many of the former Confederate officials left their jobs for the last time. Anarchy became rampant throughout the State as all authority disappeared ... until the Union army occupation.

The Civil War ended with a final gasp in Texas on May 15th 1865. The last battle of the Civil War was a land battle at Palmetto Ranch near Brownsville. Unbelievably, the battle came more than a month after General Robert E. Lee had surrendered to General Ulysses S. Grant at Appomattox Court House in Virginia.

Texas cavalry and artillery battalions commanded by Colonel John S. "Rip" Ford, along with troops such as Captain John Littleton of Karnes County, made the last battle of the war a resounding Confederate victory. [143] However the die was already cast, and this victory could not change the reality of the South's defeat. A few days after the battle, Ford disbanded his command and sent his troops home.

General E. Kirby Smith surrendered the Trans-Mississippi on June 2, 1865 At Galveston with no army left to command. Only a few weeks after, on June 19 Union troops commanded by General Gordon Granger landed in Galveston. General Granger ended slavery in Texas by issuing an order that the Emancipation Proclamation was in effect throughout the State of Texas. The Texan emancipation date is celebrated across the country as Juneteenth.

Chapter 17: Civil War Reconstruction

Upon the defeat of the Confederacy and the occupation of Texas in the summer of 1865 a number of questions remained unanswered. The two key questions facing the U.S. Congress and Lincoln's successor, President Andrew Johnson, were; How would southern states be readmitted to the Union? How would the newly freed slaves be assimilated?

After the assassination of President Lincoln by John Wilkes Booth, a reputed K.G.C. agent, there was a rage throughout the north and calls for vengeance against the defeated Confederate states. Before his assassination Lincoln had a quite moderate and lenient plan for the readmission of the former Confederate states. However after his assassination moderation and leniency for the rebel states were no longer in the cards.

President Andrew Johnson, a southerner, appointed A. J. Hamilton Governor of the state under his plan for reconstruction. He enacted a relatively lenient plan for the reconstruction in the former Confederacy. [144]

His plan was for a convention process with provisional governors presiding over individual states to repeal secession ordinances, frame a new constitution and nullify the war debt. Voters in each of these states would then adopt the convention results and elect a governor and legislators who, in turn, would ratify the 13th Amendment to the U.S. Constitution.

According to this plan elections were held in 1866 in Texas for state officials and a new state constitution. In these elections the conservative J. W. Throckmorton was elected as Governor of the State of Texas. [145]

The Texas Constitutional Convention of 1866 tried to get by with the bare minimum of requirements for readmission to the Union. They gave newly freed male slaves the right to acquire and transmit property, to sue or be sued, to contract and be contracted with, to obtain equal criminal prosecution under the law and to testify orally in any case involving another African American.

However the 1866 Constitution did not allow African Americans to hold public office or to vote. This 11th Texas Legislature meeting in August, 1866 refused to ratify either the 13th Amendment, which abolished slavery, or the 14th Amendment, which granted citizenship to African Americans. The legislature clearly tried to turn the clock back to a time before the war by restricting the rights of African Americans ... definitely a deal breaker for the victorious Yankees.

In late 1866 an anti-Johnson U.S. Congress was elected. They quickly passed the First Reconstruction Act in March 1867. So began the era of Congressional Reconstruction in which the law essentially wiped out the newly elected governments in the ten southern states. These states were then grouped into five military districts with Texas and Louisiana being placed in the fifth military district. Essentially Texas and the other former Confederate States were to be placed under the boot of the victorious Union Army ... and it was definitely pay-back time! [146]

Essentially from this point forward the former white slave owners, Confederates and sympathizers became less than second class citizens. In their opinion the newly emancipated former slaves were now their masters ... virtually overnight. The former slaves along with the radical Republicans, northern carpetbaggers and "scallywags" (a white southerner who supported the Republican Party) were now in total control.
[147]

Using the power of the occupying Union troops, they controlled every aspect of the white former Confederate men, women and children's' lives and well being. This was the beginning of the second Civil War.

Figure 11. 1872 cartoon depicting a carpetbagger

Clearly not everyone in Texas and the former Confederacy were unhappy with the victory of the Union and the new Reconstruction Government. The emancipated African Americans were ecstatic that the inhuman system of slavery had been crushed and they were now to be treated like human beings. Here is an actual statement from a slave who achieved his freedom in San Antonio.

FELIX HAYWOOD REMEMBERS THE DAY OF JUBLIO [148]

Felix Haywood, born a slave in Raleigh, North Carolina, gained his freedom in San Antonio, Texas, in the summer of 1865 when word finally reached Texas. In this interview Haywood recalls the day of emancipation.

Soldiers, all of a sudden, was everywhere—coming in bunches, crossing and walking and riding. Everyone was a-singing. We was all walking on golden clouds. Hallelujah!

Union forever

Hurrah, boys, hurrah!

Although I may be poor,

I'll never be a slave—

Shouting the battle cry of freedom.

Everybody went wild. We felt like heroes, and nobody had made us that way but ourselves. We was free. Just like that, we was free. It didn't seem to make the whites mad, either. They went right on giving us food just the same. Nobody took our homes away, but right off colored folks started on the move. They seemed to want to get closer to freedom, so they'd know what it was—like it was a place or a city. Me and my father stuck, close as a lean tick to a sick kitten. The Gudlows started us out on a ranch. My father, he'd round up cattle— unbranded cattle—for the whites. They was cattle that they belonged to, all right; they had gone to find water 'long the San Antonio River and the Guadalupe. Then the whites gave me and my father some cattle for our own. My father had his own brand - 7 B)--and we had a herd to start out with of seventy.

We knowed freedom was on us, but we didn't know what was to come with it. We thought we was going to get rich like the white folks. We thought we was going to be richer than the white folks, 'cause we was stronger and knowed how to work, and the whites didn't, and they didn't have us to work for them any more. But it didn't turn out that way. We soon found out that freedom could make folks proud, but it didn't make 'em rich.

Did you ever stop to think that thinking don't do any good when you do it too late? Well, that's how it was with us. If every mother's son of a black had thrown 'way his hoe and took up a gun to fight for his own freedom along with the Yankees, the war'd been over before it began. But we didn't do it. We couldn't help stick to our masters. We couldn't no more shot 'em than we could fly. My father and me used to talk 'bout it. We decided we was too soft and freedom wasn't going to be much to our good even if we had a education."

Now here is a totally different point of view from a white Texan who was an eye-witness to the post Civil War Reconstruction in Leon County. He clearly still retained his racial bias in 1902. [149]

'The reconstruction legislation of the Federal Congress deprived the great mass of the white people of the Confederate States, for the time being, whether so designed to or not, of all political control and transferred the same to the Federal military authorities, the ignorant negro, and the carpet-bagger.

The reconstruction laws disenfranchised a large number of the people of each of the rebel States. Not only did this legislation disenfranchise many of the white people of the Confederate States, but it put the ballot and the right to hold office into the hands of the recently emancipated slave , and delivered the white people of the rebel States absolutely into the power of the military.

The military was clothed with the legislative, executive and judicial authority. The Confederate States presented the spectacle of a free and intelligent people, in the twinkling of an eye deprived of all political authority, and their newly freed and ignorant slaves placed in power over them. These slaves to whom was given an authority over the lives and property of the whites, had no intelligence, no experience, and no more capacity for the exercise of the ballot and the powers of intelligent and just government than the mules they drove for their former masters. This reconstruction legislation so drastic and unprecedented, came unexpected, and fell with stunning force on the people of the Confederate States.

Under the State governments established in the rebel States, the creatures of reconstruction legislation of the Federal Congress, many ignorant and corrupt men obtained office, in order to have better opportunity to serve their own interest and greed, regardless of the rights and interests of the people. To such extent did this evil obtain that these governments in many instances, instead of conserving the rights of person and property, and protecting the accumulations of honest industry and thrift became engines of oppression, pillage and robbery; and it became a matter of self-preservation to the vast majority of the white people to oust these official vampires and put in office, in their stead, men of integrity and intelligence who were identified in interest and sympathy with the hopes and desires of the great mass of the people.

Chief among the troubles that came in the train of reconstruction to plague the people of Texas, none were fraught with greater evil than the Freedman's Bureau and the Loyal League. The originators of these organizations intended them to nurture, educate and solidify the Southern negroes to the interest of the Republican Party and perhaps as an incident, they intended them to protect the negro against imposition by the Southern whites, who they mistakenly supposed were the natural enemies of the negro.

Whether this was so or not, the corrupt influences that crept into both of these organizations resulted in the indiscriminate robbery of the negro and the white man. In a short time after the advent of the League, the negroes throughout Leon County were gathered into it. The negroes at once became insulting and impudent in their intercourse with the whites, and much excited over the assurance given them by the white League leaders that they would, in a short time, receive from the government forty acres of land and a mule. Many of the negroes were so confident of receiving this bounty that they mentally selected forty acres they would take, and the particular mule belonging to their former master. It was not long before parties came along who represented to the negroes that they had authority to survey and set apart to them their land, which they would do for a consideration. They did a thriving business with the poor deluded negro. Through the influence of the Bureau and the League the negroes became soured, dissatisfied and hostile to the whites, and many of them abandoned their employers and their crops, refused to labor, spent their time roaming about the country, to the great alarm of the whites, especially the women and children, and seemed to think that freedom consisted of a pony, six shooter and an exemption of work. The men and women were constantly running to the Bureau Agent with complaints of violence used on them by white people, or that some white man owed them and would not pay them, or would not divide the crop fairly with them.

The whites were continually harassed with these complaints, their persons arrested and carried by the soldiers before the Bureau, and their property forcibly seized by order of the agent. "The reconstruction act of the 3rd of March, 1867, required the general in command to cause a registration of voters before the first day of September of the same year, prescribing the oath to be taken by the voter and the qualifications he must possess in order to register, also the appointment: by the general boards of registration, comprised of *three loyal citizens,* who were to be managers of the election, count the votes and make return of same to headquarters. The registration board in Leon County consisted of two white men and one negro. It was with great reluctance that the Confederates of that county went before a board, one of which was a former slave, to qualify themselves to vote. In fact, many refused to do so and remained disenfranchised.

Of the voting population of Leon County, there were about two whites to one negro, but so many of the whites refused to register, and many were disqualified from registering, that the negroes had absolute control of the county from the time reconstruction commenced up to the election in November, 1873. At the election in November, 1869, it is evident from the vote on the constitution, which resulted for ratification 73,366 against 4928, that comparatively few of the whites were registered, or if registered did not vote.

At this election in 1869, for ratification of the constitution, the election of governer, members of Congress and all State and county officers, one of the lieutenants in charge of the Federal soldiers at Brenham, when it was burned, was sent down with a company of soldiers to supervise the election in Leon county. The polls were open for four days, and there was but one polling place in the county, and that was at Centerville the county seat. The election was held upstairs in the court house, the board of registration nominally conducting the election, but really the lieutenant in charge of the soldiers. At the foot of the stairs, he stationed three soldiers with loaded guns and fixed bayonets; at the top of the stairs he stationed two more soldiers armed as the others. He, most of the time, was seated at the table used by the election board, exercising total control over the whole matter. No one was permitted in the room during the polling but a voter, and if he was a Confederate he was told not to linger, as his presence was not needed. Through this cordon of soldiers, free-born white men had to pass to vote. It was such an indignity and such a bare-faced travesty on the freedom of elections that many of the whites who had cast aside their pride and registered refused to vote."

Below you will find the actual loyalty oath from the Journal of the Reconstruction Convention which met at Austin, Texas, June 1, A. D. 1868. Clearly this was an effective technique by the radical Republican administration to disenfranchise large percentages of whites from voting or maintaining their civil rights.

Barry H. Harrin

EVERY PERSON APPLYING FOR REGISTRATION HEREAFTER MUST TAKE
AN OATH, ETC.

Sec. 45. Every person making application for having his name entered on the registration list, shall swear and subscribe to the following oath: I —————— ——————, do solemnly swear (or affirm,) that I am a citizen of the United States, that I have resided in this State six months next preceding this day, (or, that I am a citizen of this State, that I have declared my intention of becoming a citizen of the United States, and resided in this State twelve months preceding this day,) and now reside in the county of ——————; that I am twenty-one years old; that I have not been disfranchised for participation in any rebellion or civil war against the United States, nor for felony committed against the laws of any State, or of the United States; that I have never been a member of any State Legislature, nor held any executive or judicial office in any State, and afterwards engaged in insurrection or rebellion against the United States, or given aid or comfort to the enemies thereof; that I have never taken an oath as a member of Congress of the United States, or as an officer of the United States, or as a member of any State Legislature, or as an executive or judicial officer of any State, to support the Constitution of the United States, and afterwards engaged in insurrection or rebellion against the United States, or given aid or comfort to the enemies thereof; that I have not voted as a member of any Convention or Legislature in favor of an Ordinance of Secession; that I was not a member of any secret order hostile to the government of the United States; that, as a minister of the Gospel or editor of a newspaper, I did not advocate secession, nor did I support rebellion and war against the United States; and that I will faithfully support the Constitution and obey the laws of the United States, and of this State, and will, to the best of my ability, encourage others so to do. So help me God.

Figure 12 Journal of the Reconstruction Convention, Austin, Texas, June 1, A. D. 1868.

Their total loss of power, impoverishment and realization that they were less than second class citizens made them very, very angry ... and so began a second Civil War throughout the South, in Texas and definitely in Karnes County and Helena.

Chapter 18: Civil War Reconstruction in Karnes County

As you may wonder at this point, what was Helena and Karnes County like during Reconstruction? As you will quickly see it was quite inhospitable, very angry and dangerous. Karnes County became known as one of the most lawless areas in the State of Texas.

A German immigrant who came to the town in late 1868 related that "although the regular occupation of the inhabitants was cattle raising, they enjoyed most stealing horses and looting the freight wagons which passed along the nearby road from Indianola toward inland points. He added significantly that the local authorities "had no power to check this lawlessness." [150]

The years immediately following the Civil War were a time of transition and danger for the citizens of Helena and Karnes County. They were still on the very edge of civilization and because of that they attracted some very unpleasant guests. Karnes County and its county seat of Helena were like a magnet attracting hundreds of desperados, outlaws, and former hard-core Confederates from all over the Southwest. Helena became the self-proclaimed "Toughest Town on Earth." [151]

A writer for the "San Antonio Express" newspaper in 1868 described the town of Helena as "a mean little Confed town with 4 stores, 4 whiskey mills and any amount of lazy vagabonds laying around living by their wits." He added that "these inhabitants own nothing, but have enough money for whiskey, tobacco and occasionally a game of monte."

The unsavory reputation Helena developed can best be demonstrated by one of the favorite pastimes of the hundreds of undesirables. This pastime was known as the "Helena Duel."

The so-called "Helena Duel" usually was initiated due to an overabundance of whiskey and testosterone. The dueling process was remarkably simple. First, the left hand of each participant was tied together with rawhide. Then each participant was given a short sharp bladed knife placed in the right hand. Both participants were then spun around until disoriented, to the amusement of the assembled rabble.

 The knives were short so vital organs could not easily be cut, therefore, bleeding from multiple cut and stab wounds was slow and entertaining for the drunken, cheering, crowds. The fights normally continued until one of the unlucky participants bled to death. The blood thirsty drunken crowds amused themselves by betting on the outcome. This was Helena's version of Las Vegas. [152]

One of the most vicious gunfighters of the Reconstruction Era was William Preston Longley, known as Wild Bill Longley. Longley was destined to increase the danger level in the already dangerous town of Helena. He was born on October 6, 1851 and raised in Evergreen, Texas. Wild Bill had a particular hatred of Yankees and the newly freed Negroes. [153]

Once the Civil War ended Texas Reconstruction radical Republican Governor E. J. Davis started a new State Police force, made up of at least one third mostly ex-slaves. Naturally, this did not sit well with the former Confederate whites.

On a chilly day in December 1866, Bill Longley and his father happened to be in Evergreen. Just at that time a black police officer, who had been drinking heavily, was riding down the street waving his pistol in the air and cussing out the local townspeople.

After the black police officer began insulting his father, Bill stepped forward and told the police officer to lower his gun. The policeman then pointed his gun at a fifteen year old Bill Longley, who killed the policeman with a single shot. Not long after Longley joined other young men and began terrorizing newly freed slaves. He killed two more freed Negroes in Lexington, Texas. [154]

After killing several other men, in order to elude the authorities, he headed west. Longley went to Karnes County and worked as a cowboy for John Reagan on his ranch just outside Helena. [155]

One day on his way back to the ranch after spending some quality time in the Helena saloons Longley was chased by a cavalry regiment. It seems that they had mistaken him for Charlie Taylor of the famous Taylor gang . After killing one of the troopers Bill escaped to Arkansas and was graced with a $1000 reward on his head by the military authorities. [156]

Wild Bill Longley finally met his maker after being hung to death in Lee County, Texas October 11, 1878. [157] This gunfighter and all around bad guy, is reputed to have killed 32 men before his execution.

Now if you think that you've seen it all ... you haven't!

Once the Civil War ended and for a period of several months, civil administration and law and order basically collapsed throughout Texas, including Karnes County. Things got so out of hand that thieves even broke into the state treasury in Austin and stole the last gold the state had left. [158]

Remember our Polish friends in Panna Maria. Well, those poor farmers were picked out for special treatment by the cowboys, desperados and ex-Confederates from Helena. They were singled out because many of the ex-Confederates and sympathizers considered them as traitors due to the large number of Poles who fought for the Union or supported it. After about six months things calmed down for the Poles ... that is until 1867. [159]

It was the spring of 1867 when all hell broke loose in Karnes County. It began when the anti Johnson U.S. Congress assumed control of Reconstruction. The Congressional plan allowed only freed Negroes and men loyal to the federal government to vote.

In each state of the south, registrars of voters were appointed in the counties to enroll all voters who could swear to the "ironclad" oath that they had never in any way supported the Confederacy. In effect these registrars were disfranchising a majority of the white voters and in their places allowing the former slaves and the detested northern sympathizers to go to the polls.

In Karnes County four registrars of voters were appointed in 1867. One of these men was a Pole named Emanuel Rzeppa and he became the object of probably the greatest hatred from the local whites. The anger of many Karnes County whites was immediate and frequently the Registrars received the brunt of the rage. However by the summer of 1867 the Poles were also targeted by the disenfranchised ex-Confederates. [160]

During the voter registration at Panna Maria in early August 1867 the first of many acts of violence and intimidation against the Poles by the ex-Confederates and cowboys had begun. The Americans galloped into the Polish village on horseback. The Americans not only abused the county registrars, but also beat two immigrants who were receiving their naturalization papers. [161]

As civilization faded it came down to survival of the fittest. This is the environment that the Polish farmers of Panna Maria found themselves. They were targeted by gangs of thieves, robbers and murderers. Whether in Karnes County or traveling to San Antonio the Poles were being victimized.

As Helena overflowed with criminals and rough gunslingers they sometimes rode to Panna Maria, after heavy drinking, to test their shooting skill. "On Sunday mornings they would be drunk and looking for girls." [162]

The cowboys would often be raising a big ruckus in Panna Maria and would not settle down. During this time the priest had to start mass with a shotgun. "When the unwanted criminals would be riding into town, the priest would shoot at them from the church's bell tower." These Helena cowboys staged several raids on Panna Maria sometimes shooting people in limbs or stabbing women with a knife. [163]

Although the Panna Maria Poles and their Catholic priests made some heroic efforts to fight back, the odds were stacked against them. A small group of farmers against large numbers of drunken cowboys and desperados was a losing battle.

As the situation escalated the Poles had their back to the wall and hesitantly decided to take action. The Poles had previously sought government help with little success. Finally in April, 1869 Fathers Bakanowski and Zwiardowski carried another petition from the people of Panna Maria to one of the military commanders at San Antonio. [164]

Accompanied by Father Barzynski and Bishop Dubuis, the two priests presented their petition. They discussed with the general the difficulties of the Poles at Panna Maria, and they requested from him the protection of federal troops. The general replied that he already knew of the problems that the Poles faced and said that he planned to send a body of troops to the County in about a month. Father Bakanowski argued, "In a month. . . . It could be too late because in this time they could kill all of us." [165]

The general made a quick decision based on the seriousness of the situation and called in the cavalry officer who was to command the federal troops to be sent to Karnes County. He asked the young officer how soon he could be ready to leave, to which the officer replied five days. Now it became a reality and the Poles of Panna Maria felt their prayers had finally been answered.

General John S. Mason from the U.S. Army Post of San Antonio had previously visited Karnes County. He strongly suggested to his superiors that a permanent company of infantry be transferred to Helena, as "there is no more lawless population in the state than that of Karnes."[166]

The U. S. Army arrived in Karnes County on April 10, 1869. They established there the Post of Helena for the suppression of "insurrection, disorder and violence." This was not the first time federal troops had to be brought to the county. There had been several previous occasions that the troops had to be rushed in to quell disturbances. The last occasion was in the spring of 1868 when fifty-nine troopers and two officers from the 35th U.S. Infantry were moved to Helena from Halletsville.

They camped in Helena for almost a month to protect registrars of voters from violence and intimidation. During their stay in Helena federal troops came under gunfire from its lawless inhabitants. In this encounter the former Confederates ambushed the soldiers as they crossed Hondo Creek on the way to arrest a local resident. [167]

The new troopers arrived in Helena in the spring of 1869 with no illusions about the possible fighting with outlaws and ex-Confederates. The Post of Helena was not physically impressive. It was located on a low hilltop next to the town of Helena. [168] An observer would consider the camp to be a temporary facility as it had rough board shelters and tents. The quartermaster stores weren't even on the Post. They were in a rented stone building in Helena.

The troopers at Helena were not raw recruits that the ex-Confederates could easily dismiss. These were seasoned soldiers who had served on the frontier at Fort Chadbourne and Fort Concho. The Calvary officer commanding the Post of Helena was Second Lieutenant William A. Thompson. [169]

There were on average three officers and fifty-nine enlisted men of Company H, 4th U. S. Calvary that established the Post of Helena on 10 April 1869. They were later joined there by Company G of the 10th U.S. Infantry on 12 August 1869. The two companies remained there together until Company H 4th Cavalry left the post for Austin on 15

January 1870. Company G 10th Infantry remained at Helena until 23 May 1870 when the post was formally abandoned. [170]

Upon arriving they immediately posted guards in Panna Maria at the church door to discourage attacks and also protected voter registrars during registration and balloting in Karnes and the adjoining counties.

A number of the other troopers served in much more dangerous pursuits, such as capturing, arresting and bringing in accused criminals to detention locations. A typical outlaw apprehended and delivered for safekeeping by federal troops at the Post of Helena was Oscar Rose, a wanted man with a three-hundred-dollar reward from McLennan County, Texas. He was arrested by Lieutenant George W. Smith in the summer of 1869. [171]

The commanders of the post in addition to their military duties were essentially the government. They could remove any civil official who would not take the oath of allegiance to the United States, or who failed to fulfill their duties, and then they could also hand pick their replacements.

When the Post of Helena was established, the civil affairs in the county were almost out of control. As an example, upon arriving in Helena Lieutenant Thompson wrote his superiors that the County sheriff had stolen $400 of county funds and was last seen leaving town with the minister's daughter. [172]

Two days later he reported to his superiors that a killing had occurred in Helena and the murderer had threatened to shoot anyone who would report the murder, and that "there was not a man in the town who had moral courage to inform me of the facts." [173]

Apparently once the Post of Helena got underway even these soldiers weren't immune from Helena's violence as seen from official U.S. Army records. Private John Carey, Co G, 10th Infantry was wounded in a quarrel, November 26th 1869 by a pocket knife which entered the left side, penetrating the abdominal cavity. He was admitted to the post hospital at Helena, Texas. Simple dressings were applied and the man was returned to duty January 16th 1870. [174]

Just over a year after the Post of Helena had been established the U.S. Army believed they had successfully restored order to the area of Karnes County. The cavalry left the post for Austin on 15 January 1870. Company G 10th infantry remained at Helena until 23 May 1870 when the post was formally abandoned. [175]

According to the Polish priest from Panna Maria, Father Adolf Bakanowski, the departing military officer from the Post of Helena had claimed the operation in Helena a success. Father Bakanowski said he was told that the U.S. Army in Helena during its stay had captured and executed one hundred fifty to three hundred outlaws [176] (sometimes stated rebels) in the area of Karnes County. This exaggerated statement for three hundred first appeared in his letter to Rome on 23 May 1870. [177]

During this extremely lawless period life was hard and dangerous. Here is how an old former slave described it.[178]

"I hauled freight between San Antonio and Port Lavaca and also Indianola, or Powder horn as it was called in Indianola when the worst yellow fever epidemic in Texas hit the town.

People died so fast they couldn't dig graves for them. They just dug a long trench on the beach north of town and buried them in it. When anyone ill with yellow fever began to spit black spit they were done for. In some cases they was put in boxes before they quit moving. I had to help take two girls off of beds and put them in boxes before they quit moving. Only the people who was living there a long time were affected. Those who were from outside like I was wasn't taken sick with the yellow fever.

When we was freighting we had to guard against robbers and cow skinners all the time. We would make a corral each night and put our steers in them to keep them safe. Cow skinners sure was bad in those days. They would kill anybody's cattle just to for the hides. I've seen thousands of carcasses on the priare north of Yorktown where the skinners had killed them.

I once seen the bodies of three men hanging from the limb of an oak tree down there who had been hanged by vigilantes. One time three vigilantes caught a man red-handed right in the act of skinning one of their cows. They killed him, cut the cow's paunch open and stuck the man's head in and then put up a sign warning other skinners that they would be done the same way."

I don't want to leave you with the impression that it was total chaos in the county and Texas. As you can see from this newspaper advertisement there was some semblance of commerce and trade being attempted. The advertisement below for a new stagecoach service through Helena, demonstrates that there were still commercial opportunities.

Figure 13 San Antonio Tri-Weekly Ledger July 20, 1866

Not everyone in Helena and Karnes County had turned to violence or destructive behavior. There were a lot of good people trying to keep business going and civilization growing in the county. The Ruckman family continued their life long quest to build Helena's commerce while men like William G. Butler, Monroe Choate and Pink Bennett began building the cattle industry of Karnes County ... virtually from scratch.

President Ulysses S. Grant proclaimed Reconstruction in Texas at an end on March 30, 1870. However, it wasn't until the election of 1873 , when Southern Democrat Richard Coke defeated radical Republican Governor E.J. Davis, that Texas Reconstruction died ... for good. [179]

What the U.S. Army and the Unionists didn't realize was that the violence wasn't really over ... it was just on a low burner. Some of the old K.G.C. members had begun morphing with hard core ex-confederates into paramilitary units that were the precursor to the KKK. The second Civil War was on and the South would win it, at the expense of African Americans and Hispanics ... at least until the civil rights movement of the twentieth century.

Chapter 19: The Taylor Gang

Josiah Taylor was the patriarch of the clan that played an essential part in the mosaic of Texas history. He was born in Virginia in 1791, got married in Georgia and then temporarily left his wife and two young children, to find adventure and treasure in Spanish Texas.

In 1813 serving as a cavalry Captain he fought in the Battle of Medina, the bloodiest battle ever on Texas soil. He was one of the few survivors of the battle. He rode over 450 miles to safety on horseback with seven battle wounds, including two bullets in his body.[180] He eventually reunited with his wife and two children in Georgia.

Once Texas was opened up for American settlement by Stephen F. Austin, Josiah returned to Texas in 1824, This time with his wife Hepzibeth. They finally settled down on Green DeWitt's grant. There they received a league of land in today's DeWitt County along the Guadalupe River not far from present day Cuero.[181]

They became Texas farmers and ranchers. Together they had six sons. William, Creed, Josiah Jr, Rufus, Pitkin and James. Although Josiah Sr. died at a young age in 1830, his children survived and prospered.

The most famous of Josiah's sons was Creed (1820–1906). Creed attended school in Gonzales. During the Texas Revolution Creed As a teenager was caught up in the patriotism of the time, fighting in a number of armed clashes including the Battles of Gonzales and Mission Concepcion.[182]

Under Ben Milam he took part in the storming of San Antonio. On hearing news of the frightening disaster at the Alamo, like everyone else, Creed rushed his family to safety during the "runaway scrape." He and his younger brother Josiah Jr. are reputed to have joined General Sam Houston and participated at the battle of San Jacinto.

He fought Indians on the frontier and was involved in fighting the Comanche's at the Battle of Plum Creek in 1840. Creed served under Jack Coffee Hays as a Ranger 1841. He saw action in a number of battles such as Bandera Pass and Salado Creek. At Salado Creek he received a serious, but not mortal wound. He also fought in the Mexican War (1846-48) in a number of battles including Buena Vista and Palo Alto. Although some historians claim that Creed may have embellished his service record, as you'll see shortly he and his family were tough as nails.

After the Texas Revolution, Creed began his own family. He went back to DeWitt County, married Nancy Matilda Goodbread and raised two sons and a daughter. His sons were John Hays (known as "Hays") born in 1836 and Phillip G. (known as "Doughboy" or "Doboy") born in 1837. These two boys under daddy's supervision would be future leaders of the infamous Taylor gang. [183]

After Creed's wife died he initially moved to a ranch in Wilson County near Ecleto Creek where he raised cattle and horses. Later he bought another ranch, this one in Karnes County, also along the Ecleto near Helena. [184]

Creed and his brother Pitkin became the heart of the Taylor gang and first began causing concern to South Texas authorities in the 1850s. The gang developed extensive cattle operations in DeWitt, Gonzales, Karnes, Kimble and Wilson counties.

In the aforementioned counties so called vigilance committees were formed by neighboring ranchers as their cattle began to mysteriously disappear. The neighbors blamed the Taylors and claimed they were cattle rustlers and horse thieves ... certainly a serious offense back in the day.

The epicenter of the problem seemed to be in DeWitt County which borders Karnes County. Some of the vigilance committee members included former Texas Ranger Joe Tumilson, James "Jim" Cox and our old friend, former sheriff and Indian fighter John Littleton. [185] In order to counter these seasoned vigilance committees Creed and his gang brought in hired gunfighters and increased their force to near eighty men. This essentially created a standoff allowing the Taylors to continue their questionable activities throughout the Civil War period.

As previously demonstrated the secession and Civil War period in Karnes and the surrounding Counties was a time of great animosity and violence. Staunch southerners like the Taylors were quick to take action against any Yankees or Union sympathizers and they didn't have long to wait. Word got back to the Taylors that there was a problem in Karnes County. An old man named Riddle owned a mill and had refused to grind corn for supporters of the southern cause, including women whose husbands were away fighting for the Confederacy.

Pitkin Taylor was incensed. Leading a pro-Confederate group (K.G.C.?), he found Riddle and lynched him as he begged for his life. [186] This made a lasting impression on any people in Karnes and the surrounding counties who were less than enthusiastic about the southern cause.

Although the Taylor's claimed great love for the Confederacy it appears that these bad boys used the conflict as a cover for achieving significant profits from cattle rustling and stealing horses ... and then blaming these dastardly deeds on Confederate deserters, Indians and Mexican desperados.

Now clearly I'm not trying to convince you that Karnes County and South Texas was a kindergarten. It had an overabundance of outlaws and desperados who were murdering, robbing and stealing cattle and horses. However it appears that the Taylor gang had a significant role in destabilizing Karnes County and the entire region.

As you may remember from earlier chapters regarding the Spanish period in Karnes County and South Texas, Hispanics had created very large cattle ranches in the area. After Mexico won its independence in 1821 the Spanish were overthrown and left for good. However because of weak Mexican Government control from far away Mexico City these large cattle ranches eventually fell into disrepair and the cattle ran wild.

By the time the Civil War ended in 1865, after running wild and reproducing at will for so many years the longhorn cattle may have numbered up to five million.[187] Travelers passing through the area at that time claimed the cattle were so numerous that you could never lose sight of them. After the war demand for beef or beeves exploded and the Taylors along with William Green Butler, Monroe Choate and Pink Bennett began rounding up these wild longhorns and branding them. Then they would either drive them to regional centers or move smaller herds on the Ox-Cart Road down to the Gulf coast and ship them to New Orleans to feed the country.

As cattle became king these cattle drives made some rich. However cattle rustling became a true plague that could easily put a cattleman out of business. Simple economics drove rustling to plague levels after prices soared in 1867. In Gonzales for example prices increased from $70 to $100 a head. Although the counties required brands to be registered, the rustlers used different techniques to cover up their crimes. Sometimes they would over-brand, "brandbklott" or just say the hell with it and run the stolen cattle to the regional centers with the original brand still showing.

It was common knowledge that the Taylor's were the worst rustlers in south and central Texas. The Taylors operated like a mafia mixing both legitimate and illegitimate cattle business together. The major difference with the Taylor's was they became leaders to the disenfranchised Yankee hating rebels. Also they demonstrated no hesitation in using extreme violence against lawmen or soldiers who interfered especially if they happened to be former slaves and carpetbaggers. The Taylors were definitely a part of the second civil war that refused to accept the defeat of the south or equality for African Americans.

Creed from his ranch near Helena remained the principal leader and chief strategist of the gang even after his sons and nephews came of age.

Within just a few months of Union Army occupation of Texas, Creed's sons Hays and Doughboy came to the attention of military commanders. [188]

The Taylor gang, in addition to their day to day criminal activities harassed, attacked and sometimes killed freed people. They even attacked their schools and teachers as they considered them scum, only fit to serve white people.

They also added to their many criminal services the robbery of travelers and merchants on the San Antonio to Helena road outside Helena. In fact James Thompson (aka Jim Tope) and up to 30 Taylor gang members made life a living hell for these travelers. At times they would wear stolen military uniforms impersonating military officers and at other times impersonating civilian lawmen, silver stars on their vests and all. This allowed them to get the drop on their prey ... before they knew what hit them. [189]

The authorities were after Buck Taylor who was Creed's nephew. He was accused of multiple murders in DeWitt County near Yorktown. It seems that in September, 1865 the Eighteenth New York Cavalry was on escort duty when two of the men had to drop behind due to tired horses. The Captain sent a detachment to find them. The squad found the dead bodies of the two Cavalry men lying on the side of the road.

Letters were written to the New York Unit Headquarters in Yorktown from former Rebels in the county. The former Rebels wrote anonymous letters threatening to attack their garrison and wipe them out. Also local Unionists were written or told they would die as soon as the Yankee troops left. Naturally Buck decided it was a great time to vacation outside the area ... for an extended period of time.

As you can see here there was a general sense of mayhem and violence towards the Yankee authorities, freed slaves and carpetbaggers. Let me further prove my point to you right from the mouth of U.S. Military Cavalry Commander in the District Of Texas, none other than the soon to be famous Colonel George Armstrong Custer wrote in January, 1866 "the original secessionists ... are as much secessionists today in belief and sentiments as (they were) one year ago." [190]

He added that those former Rebels were as willing to oppose the Union government as they had been during the actual war. The colonel said that if they believed a revolt could be successful the former Confederates and their sympathizers would be in "open armed hostility" to the government. I think this helps you understand what things were like on the ground.

Before the U.S, military arrived in Helena the town and the county appeared to be under siege from the Taylor gang. Here are just a few examples:

In the spring of 1866 Hays Taylor started causing problems again. Acting as a trail boss he drove a herd, a number of them stolen, from Wilson County to Indianola through Helena for shipment to New Orleans.

After delivering the herd he and some of his men went to the nearest saloon to celebrate their good fortune. Hays was at the bar drinking when two Negro soldiers bellied up. Upset that these newly freed slaves were at the same bar as whites, Hays and these soldiers exchanged some very nasty words. Hays told them that they must "step aside" because they didn't have the right to be at the same bar with them.

One of the Negro soldiers was upset with Hays' remark. He told Taylor that he was as good as any white man and wasn't going to move. After a few minutes the soldier's attention shifted to other things. In the blink of an eye Hays pulled his six-shooter and shot both soldiers. He killed one and wounded the other, as his men drew guns and held off everyone in the saloon by threatening them with the same treatment.

Hays and his men began backing away until they reached the saloon door, where they turned and broke into a run to their horses. As they galloped out of town they split up just in case they were being pursued by a posse. [191]

Hays now on his own, headed back to Karnes County. Unfortunately he encountered a military patrol led by a Negro sergeant. Hays observed that the sergeant was riding a mule that he believed had been stolen from a family friend, George Walton of Hallettsville. Hays accused the Negro sergeant of theft.

After hurling more insults Hays drew his gun and shot the sergeant in the head. The mortally wounded sergeant got off one last shot hitting Hays in the arm. Luckily for Hays the other soldiers lost all courage after the shooting, quickly riding away. Hays stole the dead sergeant's weapon and towed the mule behind his horse.

Hays headed back to Helena, the town closest to his father's ranch. He found Creed in one of Helena's many saloons. Hays had his wounded arm in a homemade sling and told his father what happened with the troopers, after calling the sergeant and his men no- good "nig**rs," [192]

Creed angrily told his son that the sergeant's mule did not belong to their friend because the mule had been found. Creed told his son to kill the sergeant's mule and bury it in the woods so the authorities couldn't find it. Although Hays didn't want to kill such a fine mule, he finally accepted his father's advice and got rid of the incriminating evidence.

Hays then quickly left the area, staying with different friends and family to avoid charges for murdering the sergeant. Reports indicate that Hays was assisted by his cousin Joe Taylor in escaping to Monterrey, Mexico. Unfortunately Creed became homesick for his friends and family after a short time. He brazenly returned to the area where the authorities were well aware of his crimes.

In December of 1866 eight members of the Taylor gang were on the San Antonio River not far from Helena and the San Antonio-Indianola Road. About midnight they came to the house of a Tejano, broke in and robbed the man. One of the gang claimed they got $115 but it wasn't easy. It seems the man's wife was game for a fight. One of the gang bragged he made short work of her. He grabbed a butcher knife and cut the woman, leaving her severely wounded and bleeding. Then the gang hid out in Karnes County. [193]

The Taylor gang members became active again in January 1867. In the dark of night Tom Dodd and Jim Wright stole four mules from a rural wagon yard near Helena after which they fled to Gonzales County. They needed to get rid of the stolen mules before the owner had time to alert the local authorities.

Our old friend John Littleton from Helena, the former Texas Ranger, and Karnes County Sheriff, Indian fighter, war hero and rancher was fed up with the Taylor gang. He knew of the Taylors' cold blooded reputation having lost too many cattle and horses to them. After they killed Major Thompson of Fort Mason in cold blood, there was a $1,000 reward offered for each of them. Littleton joined forces with William "Bill" Stannard. The Taylors got wind of the bounty hunters' plans and Taylor spies began watching Littleton and Stannard's every move.

The Taylors laughed at how easy it was to elude local authorities and even the military but they weren't laughing about Littleton. They knew his reputation and were familiar with his tenacity. They intended to be very careful with him.

Littleton and Stannard found out they were being trailed by Taylor spies so they traveled mostly at night or together with lawmen. This worked fine until Littleton had to go to an emergency business meeting in San Antonio. He got Stannard to accompany him in order to have his back covered.

Littleton used a buggy as he had gained considerable weight and could no longer ride for extended periods by horseback. They arrived in San Antonio without incident and stayed about a week while Littleton did his business. They had no problem on the way back until about ten miles from Nackenut. Hays and Doughboy Taylor had been informed by spies as to their route and waited in ambush with their men.

All of a sudden Littleton heard the thundering hooves of the Taylor gang heading right towards him with Hays Taylor in the lead. Each of the gang members were galloping towards him with either a shotgun or a six shooter ready to fire. That was probably the last thing he ever saw.

Both Littleton and Stannard tried to reach for their weapon but unfortunately they were on the floor board. The Taylor gang shot them before they could raise their weapons. As Hays reloaded he quickly saw that Littleton was already dead as a bullet had entered the right side of his head and entered into his brain. Before he died Littleton cried out "murder" at least twice. Stannard said nothing as the bullets slammed into his body. He simply fell out of the carriage. The gang began arguing as to who fired the kill shot when Stannard moaned. Hays quickly fired a shot into Stannard's head. [194]

About a hundred posse members led by Jack Helm had been tracking the gang near the San Antonio River and Coleto Creek. Detective Bell with twenty civilians and two troopers from the fourth cavalry tracked the gang to Creed Taylor's ranch on Ecleto Creek right outside of Helena.

The posse put Creed Taylor and his family under house arrest and placed guards hidden around the house waiting for Hays and Doughboy. The next morning there was a shootout and Doughboy was hit as Hays came to help him. After killing a posse member Hays was killed by a shot in the head. Doughboy and another wounded gang member made their escape much to the frustration of the posse who had already spent the reward money ... so to speak.

Creed was arrested by the posse, given over to the military at the Helena Post, than locked up in the post stockade. He was held for a month until he convinced the commander Lieutenant Crossman that he was just a harmless old war hero from the revolution and could no longer control his grown sons. The commander bought the story and freed Creed. [195]

Chapter 20: The Taylor-Sutton-John Wesley Hardin Feud

Just when it seemed like things in South Texas couldn't get worse ... they did. The Taylors became involved in a battle to the death with an opposing faction. In most history books this battle was called the Taylor-Sutton feud.

The Taylor-Sutton feud began in Dewitt County after the Civil War. It may have started over seemingly mundane issues such as disputes over cattle ownership, water rights and land boundaries but it evolved into the bloodiest feud in Texas history and lasted three decades.

This was a time in South Texas when outlaws were running amok, countered only by lawmen and vigilante groups who may have been little better than the outlaws except they had badges with their guns.

The two feuding factions were the pro-Southern Taylors, led by patriarch Creed Taylor and the pro-Union Suttons led by William "Bill" Sutton, a Dewitt County deputy sheriff and his chief enforcer, Jack Helm, a former captain of the pro-Union state police.

The Taylor-Sutton feud was the longest and bloodiest in Texas history. It lasted from the 1860s to the 1890s until the final court case mandated a state pardon for all the Texas feuds. During this period almost 200 men rode with Creed Taylor and his family against a similar force with the Sutton faction. [196]

This battle to the death affected 45 counties of Texas. However the epicenter of the violence was mainly in three counties, Dewitt, Gonzales and of course ... the always lucky Karnes County. [197]

A TEXAS VENDETTA.

HISTORY OF THE TAYLOR-SUTTON FEUD.

NINETEEN HOMICIDES ALREADY—OUTSIDE PARTIES DRAWN IN, AND A FIGHT IN-VOLVING A THOUSAND IMMINENT.

The New York Times
Published: October 5, 1874
Copyright © The New York Times

Figure 14 New York Times headline in 1874 regarding Taylor-Sutton feud

During this period the state police had a brutal reputation as being outlaws with Yankee badges. The fact that more than a third of them were former slaves just added gasoline to the fire of southern hatred. In April 1868 alleged horse thieves Charles Taylor and James Sharp were shot down in Bastrop County allegedly attempting to escape? During this period many men were killed "while attempting to escape."

The straw that broke the camel's back was the killing on Christmas Eve 1868 of Buck Taylor and Dick Chisholm by William Sutton.[198] This final spark ignited the gasoline as an orgy of violence exploded across South Texas.

After the murder of two more of their soldiers the military joined the hunt for the Taylors along with the state police and vigilantes. The state police committed acts that were not condoned by their superiors in Austin and it was at this point that the Taylors needed more muscle.

John Wesley Hardin (1853-1895) was related to the Taylors through marriage and joined them before his twenty-first birthday in 1873. He immediately became a leader and a major enforcer for the gang. Hardin had a nasty reputation as a vicious killer and gunslinger. His entry into the war certainly changed the balance of power in the Taylor's favor.

Hardin grew up in the Reconstruction era when corrupt politicians and police, backed by the United States Army treated southern women and Confederate veterans like dirt. Like many other southern young men of his generation he had a special hatred for freed slaves who went from slave to virtual master overnight, protected by Yankee guns. In Hardin's own biography he claimed he put a few men in their place while sending a few others home to the Lord. This is the angry world Hardin lived in. [199]

At the age of 14 Hardin apparently had some anger management issues and stabbed a classmate during recess. In 1868 at the age of 15 John Wesley Hardin killed his first victim, a former slave, twice Hardin's size. Under the Reconstruction laws and military justice, killing a black man was a virtual death sentence for a white southerner ... even in self defense.

Hardin later claimed to have killed three Union soldiers sent to arrest him. A combination of relatives and neighbors helped him bury the bodies to hide evidence of his complicity in the crime.

He quickly left the area, went out on his own, developing gambling skills and a love for horse racing. Hardin later admitted that by the end of 1869 he had killed a freedman and four soldiers. In December of that year he killed Jim Bradly in a fight after a card game. From this point forward Hardin fell into a never ending pattern of saloons, gambling, fighting and killing.

In 1871 Hardin joined a cattle drive to Abilene, Kansas where he had no hesitation in using his gun. He left behind a large body count. One Indian who shot an arrow at him ... and missed and five Mexicans who crowded his herd and then foolishly argued with this "kid." In Abilene Hardin both got friendly with and sparred with Wild Bill Hickock. Hardin convinced Hickock to let his cousin Mannen Clements escape from jail after he had killed two of his cowboys. However, Hardin figured he overstayed his welcome with Hickock after he shot dead a man in an adjoining room ... for snoring too loud.[200]

Hardin took a short hiatus from his life of spreading murder and mayhem and returned to Gonzales County, Texas. He got married on February 29, 1872 to his sweetheart Jane Bowen from Karnes County near Helena. She would stand by his side until her death in 1892.

Not long after entering the fray John Wesley Hardin became a hero and savior to the Taylor gang. His claim to fame was the assassination of Jack Helm. Helm was the sheriff of Dewitt County, the former Captain of the hated state police, and chief enforcer for the Sutton faction.

The assassination took place by the blacksmiths' shop at a village in Wilson County. While Hardin and Jim Taylor were at the blacksmith having a horse shod, Helm allegedly advanced on Taylor with a knife, only to be cut down by a Hardin-administered shotgun blast from behind. As Helm writhed on the ground, Taylor marched over with his pistol drawn and emptied it into Helm's head. [201]

The next night Hardin and other Taylor gang members surrounded a ranch house belonging to the Sutton ally Joe Tumlinson (In the attached military letter Tunilinson is pleading for help as he hides in the woods). A short lived truce was arranged and both sides signed a peace treaty in Clinton, Texas (DeWitt County). However in less than a year the war broke out again between the two sides.

It finally came to a head on March 11, 1874 when Jim and Bill Taylor gunned down William Sutton and Gabriel Slaughter as they boarded a steamboat with their wives at the port of Indianola. An interesting side note is that, William Sutton and his family were leaving Texas forever, before he was murdered ... in front of his family. [202]

Post of Helena, Karnes Co. Texas.

June 22 nd. 1869.

Captain Elias E. Morse, U. S. A.

A. D. C. an Secretary for Civil Affairs.

Fifth Military District.

Austin, Texas.

Captain:

I have the honor to report, that Hays Taylor, Doughboy Taylor and Ed. Glover, desperadoes, have organized a band numbering twenty-five (25) men, composed of thieves, murderers, &c. for the avowed purpose of liberating two men by the name of Woffords, now in Confinement at the Clinton Jail; and also, to Kill Mr. Tomlinson of Karnes County, Mr. Col. White & Sutton of De Witt County. These men have been driven from their homes and are now living in the woods, and do not dare to approach their homes through fear of being Killed.

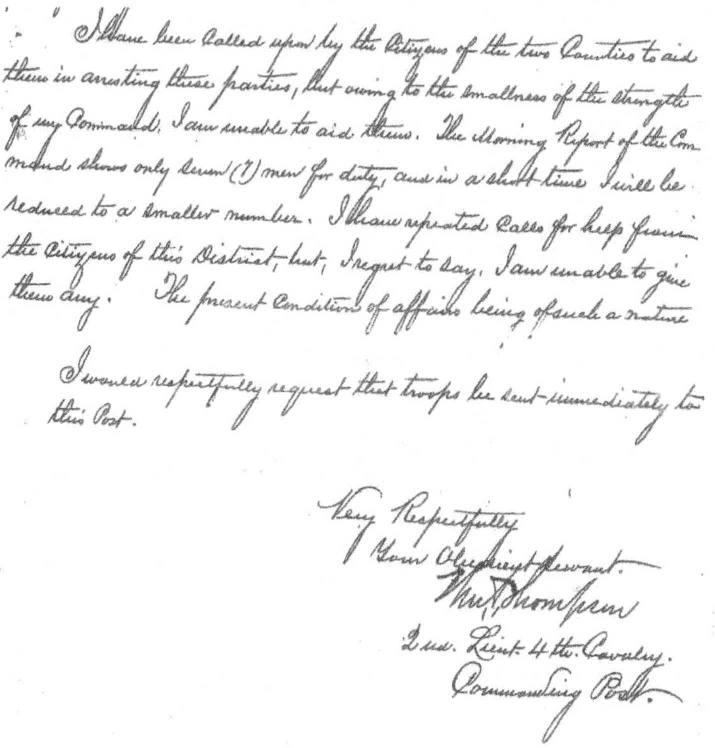

[handwritten letter]

" I have been called upon by the Citizens of the two Counties to aid them in arresting these parties, but owing to the smallness of the strength of my Command; I am unable to aid them. The Morning Report of the Command shows only seven (7) men for duty, and in a short time I will be reduced to a smaller number. I have repeated Calls for help from the Citizens of this District, but, I regret to say, I am unable to give them any. The present Condition of affairs being of such a nature

I would respectfully request that troops be sent immediately to this Post.

Very Respectfully
Your Obedient Servant.
Wm. Thompson
2nd. Lieut. 4th. Cavalry.
Commanding Post.

Figure 14 U.S. Army Post of Helena 1869-Courtesy-National Archives Washington D.C.

When Hardin went to Huntsville prison in 1878 he claimed to have killed 42 men. He was released in 1892. While in prison he attended Sunday school and studied law. He received a pardon from Governor Hogg in 1894, passed the law examination and set up practice in Gonzales. He drifted to El Paso, set up a law office there and slid back to his old ways of gambling and drinking. On August 19, 1895 John Selman with whom he had been arguing, shot him in the back of the head as he was throwing dice in the Acme Saloon in El Paso. [203]

The Taylor-Sutton feud finally ended with neither side achieving total victory. However the bottom line is that the history we were taught in school was inaccurate. Our politically correct history books were carefully cleansed and sanitized. This is especially true regarding the post Civil War Reconstruction period in Karnes County and the rest of the south.

In essence there was a second Civil War in Texas and the south and the former Confederates without any doubt ... won it. The pro-slavery Democratic Party used the Taylor gang and scores of other paramilitary groups to destroy Republican Reconstruction governments, drive out carpetbaggers and subjugate African-Americans back to near slavery levels. The Confederate victory was not overturned until the civil rights era of the 1960s ... almost a hundred years later.

Chapter 21: Helena Texas the Boom Town

Once the destructive period of Civil War Reconstruction ended in 1873 Helena and Karnes County achieved unprecedented growth and prosperity. The cattle industry was in full swing and a number of Karnes County ranchers became wealthy and powerful.

Ranchers like William Green Butler (W.G. Butler), J.M. Choate, Pink Bennett, J. M. Nichols, P. B. Butler, S.O. Porter; Buck Pettus, Edd Lott, John Wood, John Claire, Pat Burk, John Linney and John Reagan achieved wealth that would have been unthinkable, just ten years earlier. [204] America had a hunger for Texas beef, and the ranchers of Karnes County and South Texas were ready, willing and able to feed that hunger.

Helena also received a tremendous boost, due to its fortunate location on the Old Ox-Cart Road. As ships poured into the Gulf Coast port of Indianola, which now rivaled Galveston, massive quantities of goods passed through Helena on their way to San Antonio or the west.

As the economy boomed prosperity trickled down to the merchants and entrepreneurs in Helena. Many of the leading merchants such as the Ruckman's, Seidel's, Carver's and Mayfield are prospered during this period as well. [205]

From the 1870s through the early 1880s Helena was in its prime. Its streets were filled with more than 500 citizens, and this bustling little metropolis was one of the largest towns in South Texas. The majority of commercial activity and many stores were located directly across the street from the courthouse on the Old Ox-Cart Road from Indianola (now FM 81).

The Helena Record on September 5, 1879 advertised the services of four lawyers - John Baley, T.S. Archer, L.S. Lawhon and L.H.

Brown.[206] Below is an actual portion of a tax collection letter sent by the Lawyer L. H. Brown to Misters Hutchinson and Franklin in San Marcos, Texas. Notice that Lawyer Brown was part of a nationwide collection agency ... back in 1879.

Also in the newspaper are advertisements for physician and surgeon, Dr. J.W. Harmon. Proprietors Hoff and Meyer of the Pearl Saloon ran the following ad that day: "Keeps constantly best kind of liquors and segars (sic). With polite and attentive barkeepers, Recherche Liquors and Cigars that are Bon, we cannot but please the taste of the ton." General store owner Max Cohn boasted of a new addition, a furniture store, which had "long been wanted in Helena."

The little city of Helena was also a chief stop on the stagecoach route connecting San Antonio, Goliad and the Gulf Coast port of Indianola with four-horse stages passing through town daily.

Figure 15 Helena, Texas possibly in 1870's (Courtesy Sykes Mclain Historic Collection)

Helena, the county seat, had a courthouse, a jail, a Masonic lodge, a drugstore, a blacksmith shop, a livery stable, a harness shop and churches. There were also two newspapers. The first was the Helena Record that began publication in 1879 with the motto "Don't Tread on Me." and the second newspaper was the Karnes County News first published in 1887. [207]

In 1867, Charles Russell, A.J. Trueman, and John Ruckman organized a joint stock company for the purpose of creating a coeducational college, the Helena Academy. In 1872 the Helena Academy was built by private subscription and fifty-five citizens contributed twenty-five dollars each or donated livestock rather than cash. It is interesting to note that among the stockholders, two subscribed $25.00 by each giving two beeves and one individual subscribed the equivalent of one share with $25.00 in bacon. [208]

Figure 16 The Helena Academy- Courtesy Karnes County Museum Helena, Texas

Donors included, Pink Bennett, John Ruckman, Thomas Ruckman, Elder, Sullivan, Bill Mayfield and Al Mayfield. The two-story rock structure housing this "male and female institution of the highest order" was completed in 1872 and soon enrolled thirty-five girls and even more young men. Males and females were taught on separate floors. The college operated until the mid-1890s when the old rock structure was used to store corn for a few years before burning down.
[209]

In 1873, a rock courthouse was built. A bell and belfry were added after 1895 when it was converted into a school. The second floor of the courthouse has witnessed an untold number of hard fought trials. Too many of them ending with some unlucky participant swinging from one of the two "hanging trees" near the courthouse. It is said that on trial days crowds of people would bring their whole family with a picnic basket, in the hope of seeing some biblical justice.

Speaking of biblical justice, it seems that Helena was home to a biblical cult that received international attention. Here is an article from the "The Christian Life Volume 6, 1880, London, England. "America is a place of marvelous originality and invention. Dr. Tanner is already out of date. Another man equally wise has the field. He firmly believes that a second flood will come next November to cover the whole face of the Earth, and is building an ark at Helena, Texas. The craft will hold fifty persons, with food for forty days and forty nights, and he will take passengers at $500 each. Every other vessel, he explains, will be wrecked. We must be off to Texas." [210]

Figure 17 One of the earliest known pictures of the Courthouse, possibly 1870's-Courtesy Karnes County Museum Helena, Texas

Naturally, any good courthouse needs a good jail. Helena got its jail several years after the courthouse was built. It was a two story stone building filled with iron cells, one of which can still be seen in the courthouse square today. The building itself was torn down and moved to Karnes City and rebuilt. It later served as the Jauer store building.

Figure 18 Helena jail cell-Picture courtesy Brian Harrin

Previous to this, the jail was an iron cell, 10' by 10' built by Z. King and Son Company of Cleveland Ohio. Completed in January 1876 the structure cost $2,200. Before that facility was available the sheriff routinely took prisoners to the blacksmith to be fitted with irons that allowed them to be fastened for safekeeping. [211]

The first real church was the Helena Union Church built in 1866. It was used by Methodists, Presbyterians and Baptists who alternated holding services there. Previous to this worship services had been held in the blacksmith shop, the courthouse and any other place available. The old church, was blown down by a hurricane in 1973, was then carefully dismantled and the pieces stored for future restoration.

Figure 19 Old Union Church Helena Texas- Courtesy Karnes County Museum Helena, Texas

In 1873 an iron bridge replaced the rickety old wooden one. For a number of years after this it was a toll bridge [212] until the county finally took it over. Legend has it that the bridge was a favorite meeting place for young couples seeking a romantic encounter.

Thomas Ruckman's younger brother, John Ruckman, married in 1867, certainly a difficult period for Helena residents. He married Eliza Dickson whose family had moved to Helena from Arkansas. They eventually had eight children.

In 1878 John Ruckman must have been doing well financially as he built a showplace home in Helena. It was a three-story, six-bedroom mansion. The house was constructed of Florida cypress shipped by schooner from Florida to the port of Indianola then transported up the Ox-Cart Road by wagon and team to Helena. [213]

Ruckman's home was the town's social center. Circuit preachers always stayed there and the largest room in the Ruckman house, the family dining room, was usually full of out-of-town guests and ranch hands. The Ruckman house still stands today not far from the court-house.

Figure 20 John Ruckman House- Courtesy Karnes County Museum Helena, Texas

Now, I don't want to give you the impression that all that prosperity had turned Helena into a center of culture and civility, because that's just not the case. The 1870s and 1880s were certainly better than the near anarchy of the Civil War and Reconstruction eras, but there were definitely issues. One of those issues was still cattle rustling.

In March 1875 W.G. Butler had a serious run-in with some unsavory characters. The problem began on a bright moonlight night, when an outlaw by the name of Frank Fountain and about thirty of his gang rode silently into the area of the San Antonio River and Escondido creek.

The gang fanned out up the creek about five miles and rounded up all the cattle they could find. By the time the sun rose the next morning the rustlers had herded about 9,000 head of cattle. They all came together a few miles from where the town of Kenedy is now located and began driving them to the west. After driving the cattle hard for a day they came to Atascosa Creek in Atascosa County at what was then Peacock Ranch.

After a local cattleman came upon the stolen herd he noticed the brands were from Karnes County. He rode hard to the Conquista crossing on the San Antonio River where he knew W.G. Butler was camped, reaching there about sunup. Butler sent riders to alert all the cattlemen in the area to meet at his camp with good horses and weapons. At eight o'clock that night they all met at Butler's camp at the Conquista crossing, five miles below where Fall City is now located. One of the riders who happened to be with Butler was a young man by the name of Fate Elder. Remember his name as he would one day be Sheriff of Karnes County.

Butler and his posse rode hard for less than an hour before they struck the trail of the stolen herd which was easy to do in the bright moonlight. After riding all night long they stopped to get some sleep and let the horses rest and graze. They wasted little time resting and were back riding by sunrise. After going up a high hill they looked down and saw a large herd of cattle about a mile away.

Butler consulted with his small force of ten men as they checked their pistols. Butler and his men only numbered ten versus Frank Fountain and his thirty rustlers, who had a vicious reputation. In spite of this and their fear of the violent outcome, Butler was chosen leader of the party and, with their hearts pounding in their chests, they all rode together into the stolen herd.

Mr. Butler rode up beside Mr. Fountain and said to him, "My name is Butler and I understood that you have some of our cattle in your herd, and that you have said that you would not allow your herd to be cut. We have come to cut our cattle." To this Fountain replied, "Mr. Butler, you or anyone else who have cattle in any herd can cut them out. "

Fountain ordered his men to bunch the cattle. Butler's men cautiously proceeded to cut out 2,700 head, with one eye on the thirty armed rustlers, who appeared none too pleased about losing their bounty. However, under Fountain's orders they allowed the ranchers to cut their herd with the understanding they could return the next day to cut the balance from the herd.

They drove their 2,700 cattle about a mile away and stopped them for the night, taking turns guarding the cattle. About noon the next day they cut the balance of 1,800 from the rustlers' herd then began driving their 4,500 cattle back home. Along the way they met up with a number of cattlemen from Bee and Atascosa Counties who, thanks to Butler, were able to recover most of their cattle, too. [214]

Another issue for Helena was the large number of saloons that were filled on weekends with rowdy cowboys, teamsters, drivers and some nasty outlaws and gunslingers. The outlaws and gunslingers came to Helena from all over Texas and the southwest, as they appeared to be comfortable there.

Figure 21 Helena Street Scene 1879-1884-Courtesy Karnes County Museum Helena, Texas

However, it wasn't just the outside rustlers, desperados and gunslingers like the Taylor gang or John Wesley Hardin who brought mayhem. Sometimes, even native sons of Helena and Karnes County could cause deadly violence ... after too much whisky.

Wealthy rancher and cattleman W.G. Butler had twin brothers, George Washington Butler and Marquis Lafayette Butler. In 1879 at 28 years of age they were known as Wash and Fate. Clearly the Butler men had a well-deserved reputation for being hard-headed and the type of men you didn't push too far ... unless you were looking for serious trouble.

It was August 4th, a typical hot Texas day, when Wash and a friend John Cooper rode into Helena for some serious drinking and hell-raising. As the alcohol flowed freely and mixed with male testosterone, the two men began to argue. The argument spilled from the saloon into the streets of Helena where the two men shot each other to death in a dramatic gunfight. [215]

Unfortunately ... this would not be the last tragedy to impact the Butler family.

Chapter 22: The Daileyville Massacre

The Daileyville massacre makes the Shoot-Out at the O.K. Corral look like a Sunday school picnic. In the span of less than two minutes, five men fell mortally wounded (Three lawmen and two civilians). At Daileyville there were more people involved, more shots fired, and more dead or wounded than at the O.K. Corral. [216] This ambush was a premeditated assassination of lawmen, planned for eighteen months, by a powerful rancher ... for the killing of his son in Helena.

First let's understand the background of Daileyville before we discuss the tragedy. Once Karnes County was established in 1854 with Helena as its county seat by Judge Thomas Ruckman and Dr. Lewis Owings, the citizens had a problem. In the beginning the citizens of Helena had to cross the San Antonio River at Wofford Crossing and proceed all the way to Goliad to get their mail.[217] After awhile approval was received to operate a post office in Helena. Naturally this was a real convenience for the people of the new Karnes County and a point of great pride.

Daileyville was created to fill a need. After the establishment of Bee County in 1857 it became necessary to build a road to connect Helena with Beeville, the county seat of Bee County. A state road and a mail route were built to fill this need. The new road branched off the Helena-Goliad road on the west side of the San Antonio River near Wofford Crossing and then meandered south to Beeville. [218]

Then in 1869 soon after the Civil War David Dailey and his brother Christopher P. Dailey opened a general store on this Helena-Goliad road where the Beeville road branched to the south. Their small village of Daileyville was located on the west side of the San Antonio River only a short distance from the river and Wofford Crossing. This village would have been on the old Pleas Butler's "33 Ranch." It had the Dailey's general store, a grist mill, possibly a cotton gin and several houses.

A post office was approved with C. P. Dailey as the first postmaster. The post office was in service from July 5, 1870 until May 27, 1884 when the store closed. The store was re-opened in November 1885 but it was never again a post office for Daileyville.

It appears there was a sense of normalcy and civilization before the Daleyville tragedy. This is from an 1880 medical journal. [219]

Gentlemen: Please send me per "Pacific Express" the drugs mentioned below. I will say here that your "specific medicines" give me better satisfaction than any drugs I have ever used. I have been using yours over four years. They stand the test and always fit the bill. W.D. Matney M. D. Daileyville Texas February 28th 1880.

Figure 22 The Daileyville General Store Built in 1869-Courtesy Institute of Texan Cultures

This wooden general store and post office building was a central prop in the Daileyville tragedy. It was directly in the line of fire on September 6, 1886 and many bullet holes could be identified in its walls in subsequent photographs. The building was dismantled in 1887 and rebuilt in Kenedy serving as its first post office, with C. P. Dailey as postmaster.[220] Interestingly Dailey had been postmaster in the Confederate post office in Helena as well as the one in Daileyville and finally Kenedy.

The massacre, or as some have called it, the fracas at Daileyville took place on September 6, 1886. On this momentous day an election was to be held at Daileyville in Precinct 4 for the southern portion of Karnes County.

The election would determine whether saloons would be allowed (wet) in the southern part of the county, or not (dry).

This was a contentious election with two major factions. On one side was Karnes County Sheriff Fate Elder who favored a "dry" vote. On the other side was the powerful and wealthy rancher William G. Butler (WGB), who favored a "wet" vote.

Now to make matters worse there was bad blood between these men and their families. WGB believed that Sheriff Elder and his men had been harassing the Butler family.

However it is believed there was an issue much worse and at a much deeper level that was eating away at WGB. This issue was the fact that twenty months earlier Fate Elder had fired some of the shots that ultimately killed WGB's son in Helena, when Fate was deputy sheriff. After Edgar Leary was shot dead by WGB's son, Fate was appointed Karnes County sheriff.

After the tragedy at Daileyville there was an inquest. At that time Dr. S. G. Dailey testified that "the Elders and the Butlers were sooner or later going to have a difficulty, because the Elders were so abusive toward them that a fight would be the result of it."

The reason I choose to call this tragedy on September 6, 1886 a massacre is because it was not a shootout ... it was a planned and premeditated shooting. It has been estimated that 75 bullets targeted the unsuspecting lawmen in less than 2 minutes while they barely got off 7 shots in return.[221]

What follows next is how this terrible incident unfolded that fateful day according to the sworn testimony given at the Justice of the Peace Inquest, murder trials and newspaper articles. Please note that as pointed out by Archie Ammons in his book "Karnes County Texas Gunfights" that when reading the original testimony at the inquest, a pistol is a six-shooter. A gun is a rifle or Winchester. In 1886 a pistol is NOT a gun.

As a general comment on the testimony: Many of the witnesses seemed reluctant to stick their neck out identifying the shooters and killers. They claimed that the thickness of the gun smoke prevented them from identifying who did what to whom ... and with what.

Butler's hired hands seemed to have practiced their testimony. They didn't see or do anything ... and by the way, they had left their firearms on the ground back at the ranch.

Back in the day when a town had an election, firearms were banned during that day. It appears that the WGB faction of about 17 men all gathered around a "hack" or wagon. The "hack" was owned and operated by WGB's son-in-law Andrew M. Nichols, who tied it to a tree just south of the store and voting place. [222]

It was a warm and comfortable day as two Mexican pistoleros rode up to the "hack" and tied their horses. The two pistoleros were later identified as Juan Coy and Epitacio Garza. These two men were known to be enforcers for WGB and were very excellent marksmen with their extra-long Winchesters. Clearly either bringing these rifles or pulling them was illegal. Juan Coy was known as a dangerous man who killed a Negro in Floresville in Wilson County not long before this election. His look was vicious and he was described as "... one of the ugliest living at the time, strongly resembling a lion." He was definitely a scary looking hombre.[223]

Deputy Jack Bailey walked out to the hack and began talking with his friend Newton Butler. However it was obvious Bailey wasn't aware of what was about to occur.

Sheriff Fate Elder, who was impossible to miss, with his red hair and long red beard, was sitting in front of the store whittling on a piece of wood. He quickly got up and headed for the "hack" just behind deputy Bailey, putting up his whittling knife as he walked. [224]

Suddenly Sheriff Elder pulled his pistol after seeing WGB's Mexican enforcers with the long rifles at the ready. Juan Coy said "Stop" and then repeated "Stop" again. Elder said something unintelligible and within seconds, all hell broke loose as a fusillade of gunfire broke out.

At the inquest, several witnesses testified that the Mexicans started the shooting. Juan Coy clearly had targeted Sheriff Fate Elder and kept firing as he walked towards him. At the same time, Elder was backing away towards two mesquite trees, trying desperately to avoid the gunfire from Juan Coy's Winchester. [225]

Sheriff Elder tried to return fire twice but his pistol misfired. Unfortunately for Sheriff Elder a second assailant snuck up on his blind side, placing his pistol within about four inches of his head ... and fired. [226]

The force of the bullet slamming into Elder's head blew his hat into the air ... and Elder fell forward dead. [227] A witness at the inquest identified the second assailant as WGB's 18-year-old son Sykes Butler.

Deputy Bud Elder had been inside the voting place when he heard the first shots. He quickly ran out the front door with his pistol at the ready. However he received an unpleasant surprise as four shooters immediately began firing at him with Winchesters from a distance. Coy and Garza had just finished with his brother, Sheriff Fate Elder. They now redirected their Winchesters along with two other shooters to the stunned Deputy Bud Elder. Elder was hit several times and received a serious wound.[228]

Deputy Jack Bailey tried to get clear of the fight by running towards the yard on the east side of the store. As he ran he cried "O Lordy, Lordy, don't shoot me. I never done anything." By then he was down on his back. He repeated the plea but was shot again anyway ... in the knees.

Inside the store Deputy Vivvy Barefield was brandishing a shotgun. The storekeeper Kit Dailey, ran out the door just as Barefield fired outside the door. Buckshot hit Dailey in the foot, and he quickly returned to the store.

Some people claimed that when Dailey returned to the store, he leaped into a flour barrel for survival but Dailey testified at the murder trial that he crouched behind a sugar barrel.

Deputy Bud Elder was overheard a number of times stating that in any confrontation with the Butler's he would go for the "old man." As bullets were flying around him Bud Elder saw 52 year old WGB coming through the gate next to the store.

Bud opened fire at WGB shooting twice. As both men advanced toward each other, firing at virtually point blank range, the smoke enveloped them. One bullet severed Butler's ear and the faces of both men received powder burns. [229]

The injured Deputy Bud Elder dropped to his knees. He had fired all his rounds as did Butler. Than an unidentified man walked up and shot Elder in the head at close range. Elder was still trying to fire his pistol. He died with his pistol cocked and his finger in the trigger. Elder had been shot down to his knees by both the rifle and the pistol fire.

He had fired all his rounds and his shooting became impaired as life drained from his body. It appears that someone waited until Elder's weapon was empty before they dared shoot him in the head with a pistol at close range.

It was discovered later that Elder had been shot with more bullets than WGB's revolver would hold, clearly indicating that some of his many wounds were from multiple shooters. It doesn't appear Elder ever had much of a fighting chance.

The two brothers Henry and Hiram Pullin had been sitting on boxes next to the gate east of the store before the shooting erupted. Hiram's son Tom was leaning against the fence nearby. When it was all over

Henry was lying by the gate shot through the chest. Hiram tried to run for cover but was hit in the back by a stray bullet when he was just inside the gate. Tom had made it safely to the back of the Dailey store.

The Mexican enforcers walked calmly to the fence looking down at the seriously wounded Deputy Jack Bailey on the ground. Then they returned to their horses again stopping to look at Sheriff Fate Elder's bloody and lifeless body ... as if to check the quality of their work.

Andy Nichols the son-in-law of WGB walked out to one of the Mexicans, Epitacio Garza and shook hands with him. Coy and Garza replaced their rifles in their saddle scabbards, mounted up and rode out.

It appears that the Pullin brothers were unintended victims in the barrage of bullets. Henry Pullin had died instantly while his brother Hiram lasted a few hours.

A telegram sent to San Antonio brought Dr. Amos Graves on a special train to tend to Deputy Jack Bailey. Bailey's left knee was shattered. Dr's Graves and S. G. Bailey had to amputate his leg the next day. [230]

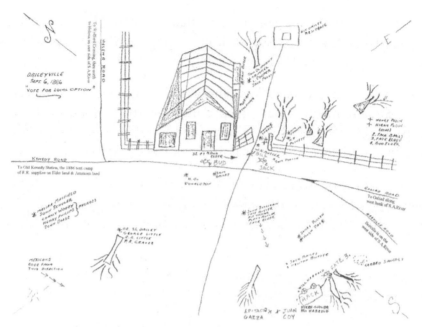

Figure 23 Old sketch of the Daileyville massacre-Courtesy Charlotte Nichols

Bailey would never speak about his assailant. When his wife asked who had shot him he whispered in her ear. Bailey died shortly after the amputation. His wife never revealed the words he had previously whispered to her.

Figure 24 Photo of a crowd in front of Dailey's General Store in the 1880's site of the Daileyville massacre-Courtesy of the Institute of Texan Cultures

Many people felt that the key to the mystery was the "hack" driven to Daileyville by Andy Nichols, WGB's son-in-law. Many people believed that under those conveniently placed feed sacks and blankets covering the seat and bed of the "hack" were the weapons used in the massacre.

Tom Pullin claimed that he had been in the back earlier in the day and no guns were to be seen. Here is an interesting side note. Thomas Nolen Pullin, a son of the murdered Hiram Pullin, was in Daileyville that day. He is the great-grandfather of the famous baseball pitcher Nolan Ryan.

As you can see below even sophisticated New Yorker's were reading about Juan Coy in the New York Times in 1886 and his part in the Daileyville massacre.

MEXICANS EXCITED.

THE EXTRADITION OF JUAN SANTOS COY FOUND FAULT WITH.

LAREDO, Texas, Oct. 10.—The large anti-American element here and Mexicans across the river in Neuvo Laredo are considerably excited over the extradition of Juan Santos Coy, whose delivery to officers of Karnes County, Texas, was reported on Oct. 8. The *Mutulista*, the most influential Spanish paper in either of the two Laredos, has a column editorial this morning denouncing what it terms the kidnaping of Mexican citizens. The *Mutulista* has a large circulation among influential Mexicans. Its attitude is likely to result in an inquiry into the case by the Government of Mexico.

According to the version of the *Mutulista*, the extradition was a clear case of kidnaping and bribery. Its facts are radically different from the story told by the Karnes County officers, who stated that the Mexican authorities surrendered Coy. The *Mutulista* says the prisoner's true name is Juan Angel; that he is a citizen of the State of Coahuila, and that Capt. Morrell and the Chief of Police in New-Laredo entered into a conspiracy with the Texas officers to capture and deliver Coy, or Angel, for a stipulated sum of money. In order to accomplish the arrest of Coy Capt. Morrell wrote him a letter telling him he was about to appoint him to a position on the police force of New-Laredo, and asking him to call at police headquarters at midnight. Coy reported promptly, and was hurried to a dungeon underneath the police station. He was kept in the dungeon two days and nights and refused permission to send for his friends or to communicate with a single person. At midnight last Thursday he was taken from his prison, and with the assistance of two American officers from Karnes County, Texas, was carried to Rio Grande and brought over to Texas in a small boat.

The *Mutulista* declares that the Americans paid $800 in gold as blood money for the delivery of Coy, or Angel. It calls upon the supreme authorities of Mexico to avenge "this outrage, this sale of a Mexican citizen."

Sheriff Sanchez, of this (Webb) county, who took part in the hunt for Coy, declares that his extradition was regular and satisfactory to the authorities of Tamaulipas. Sanchez was reticent about the payment of any money to Mexican officers. The prisoner was carried to San Antonio to-night under a heavy guard. He will be delivered to the Acting Sheriff of Karnes County in a day or two. Coy had an accomplice named Garcia in the brutal murder of Sheriff Elder, and Texas officers are making efforts to secure him. An officer is on his track in Coahuila. It is greatly feared that trouble will grow out of this matter, as the Mexicans are becoming much excited.

The New York Times
Published: October 11, 1886

No one will ever know for sure the truth of the gun battle at Daileyville, Texas. Unbelievably WGB and Sykes Butler were acquitted of murder charges.

As for the Mexican Juan Coy, it was said of him that when trouble was brewing down in Mexico he would go there "just to be in on the killing." He finally met his end at a saloon in San Antonio. Coy was unarmed at the time. The story was that after being shot he advanced on his assailant shouting "Shoot me again you SOB." A second shot rang out as Coy continued to advance and he shouted again. "Shoot me you SOB." However the third shot was answered only by silence. [231]

Today Daileyville, the site of one of the "Old West's" most violent and premeditated massacres of lawmen, no longer exists. The author, after a two year search, believes the town has now returned to its original state ... a desolate, windswept hill overgrown with prairie grass near the San Antonio River. [232]

Chapter 23: Helena's Painful Death

"The old town of Helena looks like a tree without any leaves on it since the County Seat left. Scarcely a person from outside town is seen on the streets. The boys have taken possession of the old courthouse building and last night they held a kangaroo court." [233]

After the killing of W.G. Butler's son in 1884 there was a general consensus about Helena that certainly impacted its future. This was reinforced with the news of the massacre at nearby Daileyville. Here are some quotes that will illustrate this point.

The San Antonio Reporter in 1884 wrote "The County now has an opportunity to place itself on record as a law and order place, but unless a man of courage and judgment is elected to fill the office of Sheriff, county organization ought to be abandoned, and attachment to some adjoining county for judicial purposes ought to be its fate."

Also in 1884 the supervisor of the railroad said "If the new rail line could be run around Karnes County, it would be better for everybody." Clearly, this coming from the railroad that held Helena's future in their hands was not a positive sign.

"The town in the late 70's and 80's grew to a city of considerable size, only to dwindle down and almost die after the County seat was removed to Karnes City following the building of the San Antonio and Aransas Pass Railway through the County in 1889-1890." [234]

Not long after W. G. Butler yelled "This town killed my son, now I'm going to kill this town," his revenge began. The first problem began when the San Antonio and Aransas Pass Railroad started construction through Karnes County in 1885.

The citizens of Helena had the arrogant belief that the railroad needed them as they were one of the larger towns in the area and the railroad had no choice but to give in to Helena's terms. Therefore they refused to pay a $35,000 bonus or even donate the right-of-way for a rail connection. [235]

Colonel Butler, never one to miss a good opportunity, contacted the railroad pioneer and traffic manager, Benjamin Franklin Yoakum. Butler quickly offered Yoakum a free right-of-way through his land subject to one condition: the rails had to be laid far to the west of the San Antonio River and Helena.

Judge Ruckman got wind of Butler's offer and frantically raised $32,000 but to no avail. Yoakum had accepted Colonel Butler's offer. Within a year the line was built on the other side of the river, seven miles southwest of Helena. [236]

After the railroad came through the county in 1886 the Ox-Cart Road was abandoned and two new towns, Kenedy and Karnes City, soon sprang up on the line. In 1887, Kenedy became a roundup station for cattle grazing on the open range. It was first located four miles from its present site and named for Mifflin Kenedy, a financier of the railroad. In 1892, Karnes City became a railway shipping point on the new line and within only one year it became the largest town in the county. [237]

Colonel Butler's so called curse of Helena became a reality. Soon stores, businesses, and homes began to move to Karnes City and its new rail connection. To add insult to injury, on December 21, 1893 a countywide election was held to choose a county seat.

Karnes City received 862 votes, while only 120 people wanted the county seat to remain in Helena. [238] On January 2, 1894 the Commissioners' Court ordered the county records moved from Helena to Karnes City.

Losing the election was a bitter pill to swallow for the furious residents of Helena who refused to turn over the records. A group of Karnes City men decided that the safest way to carry out the mandate of the court was to literally steal the county seat under cover of darkness.

To accomplish this they stealthily brought twenty horse-drawn wagons into Helena one night, essentially appropriating all the County records and files. As a face-saving gesture, a single guard from the now-ghost town resigned himself to riding "shot-gun" on one of the wagons. [239]

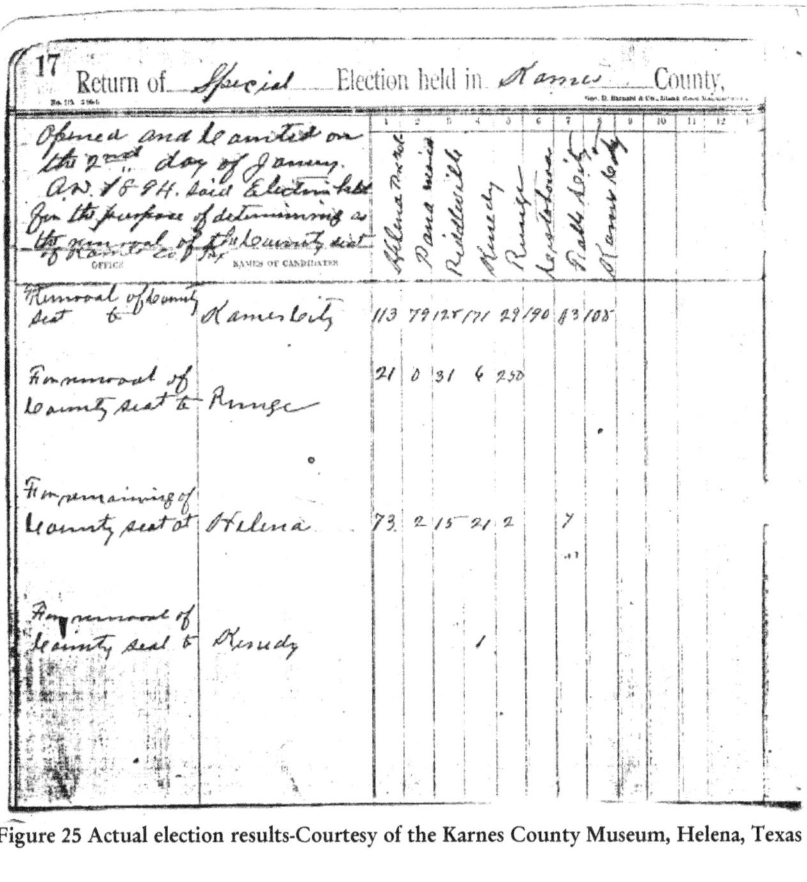
17 Return of Special Election held in Karnes County,

Opened and Counted on the 2nd day of January A.D. 1894. Said Election held for the purpose of determining as the removal of the County seat of Karnes Co.

Office	Names of Candidates								
Removal of County seat to	Karnes City	113	79	125	171	29	190	83	105
For removal of County seat to	Runge	21	0	31	6	250			
For remaining of County seat at	Helena	73	2	15	21	2		7	
For removal of County seat to	Kenedy				1				

Figure 25 Actual election results-Courtesy of the Karnes County Museum, Helena, Texas

It must have been a depressing time for those who loved Helena and had expended so much time and energy to build the town. They had courageously fought against Helena's detractors and enemies and finally had to admit defeat.

As this official letter from the Tax Assessor demonstrates, by 1896 all the official parts of county government had moved to Karnes City, the new County seat. It had to be clear to everyone that Helena's best years were behind her.

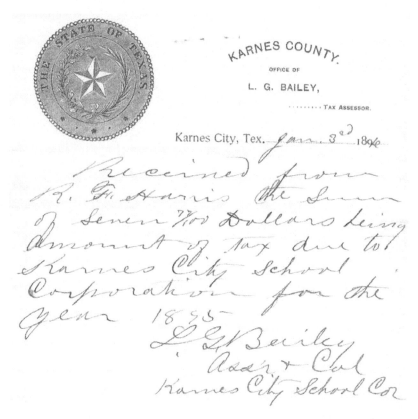

The revenge of W.G. Butler was complete. He had plunged a knife in the heart of the town that killed his son ... and then watched it fall and die!

Chapter 24: The Ballad of Gregorio Cortez

Gregorio Lira Cortez was a tenant farmer and vaquero in Karnes County Texas. After killing two South Texas lawmen in the early 1900's, he became the greatest folk hero to Tejanos, and brought terror and fear to the Anglos of Texas. Over a ten day period he reawakened an anger and courage to fight against Anglo domination, absent since the time of Juan Cortina.

During those 10 days Cortez was chased by the Texas Rangers and a posse of as many as 300 heavily armed men. Although this was one of the largest manhunts in history, he eluded them while traveling almost 400 miles on horseback and more than 100 miles on foot. To the Anglos he was a blood-thirsty murderer. To the Mexican-Americans of Texas he was a symbol in their fight against oppression and racism. [240]

In 1889 at the age of fourteen Gregorio Cortez moved to Karnes County with his older brother Romaldo. Gregorio and Romaldo worked as vaqueros, farm workers and common laborers from then until 1901. [241]

According to Texas State Prison records in Huntsville, Gregorio Cortez's height was approximately five-feet nine-inches tall, his weight was 144 pounds, his hair black and wavy , his eyes as dark brown and his complexion as "medium dark." [242]

On June 12, 1901 Karnes County Sheriff W. T. "Brack' Morris while investigating a horse theft, went to the Thulemeyer ranch outside of Kenedy where Gregorio and Romaldo Cortez were tenant farmers. [243]

Morris was 41 years old and had spent half his life in law enforcement. He was a former Texas Ranger and had been Karnes County Sheriff since 1896 and in 1901 was serving his third term. He was not a big man but had a reputation as being fast and accurate with his revolver. [244]

After Sheriff Morris discovered that Gregorio had acquired a mare in a trade with Andres Villarreal from Kenedy, Morris came out to the Cortez place seeking a horse thief described only as "... a medium-sized Mexican with a big red broad-brimmed Mexican hat. [245] He decided to question the Cortez brothers. During the questioning, there was a misunderstanding between Morris and the Cortez brothers resulting from poor translation by his Deputy Boone Choate.

Apparently the Deputy did not speak Spanish as well as he thought. Allegedly, Gregorio's brother Romaldo told Gregorio, "*Te quieren*" ("Somebody wants you"). Deputy Choate interpreted this to mean "You are wanted," indicating that he was indeed the wanted man they were after.

Choate apparently asked Cortez if he had traded a "*caballo*" ("horse") to which he answered "no" because he had traded a "*yegua*" ("mare"). A third misinterpretation

involved another response from Cortez, who told the sheriff and deputies, "*No me puede arrestar por nada*" ("You can't arrest me for nothing"), which Morris understood as "*A mi no me arresta nadie*" and translated as "No white man can arrest me... After that, things went from bad to worse, as Morris shot and wounded Romaldo, prompting Gregorio to shoot and kill Morris.

Cortez and his bleeding and feverish brother Romaldo waited in the brush until dark. They quietly made their way into Kenedy, about 9 miles away, where Gregorio left his wounded brother with the Cortez family on the outskirts of town.

Cortez, escaped by walking almost 80 miles in about 40 hours, to the ranch of Martín and Refugia Robledo on the property of Mr. Schnabel near Belmont.

Acting on a tip Gonzales County Sheriff Glover and his posse stormed the Roblado house and cornered Cortez. There was an exchange of gunfire Glover and Constable Schnabel were shot dead. Cortez was blamed for both deaths, although in the heat of battle Schnabel was called by a drunken Deputy. Cortez escaped again by walking almost a 100 miles to the home of Ceferino Flores. Flores, a friend, provided him with a pistol, horse and saddle. He then headed toward Laredo, Texas on the Mexican border.

TEXAS CHASE FOR BANDITS.

Three Americans and Three Mexicans Killed Since the Outbreak of Hostilities Nine Days Ago.

SAN ANTONIO, Texas, June 20.—Since the outbreak of hostilities in Southwest Texas between bandits and the authorities casualties have resulted as follows:

June 12—Sheriff W. T. Morris of Karnes County, in attempting to arrest Mexicans charged with horse stealing, was killed and one of his assailants wounded.

June 14.—In attempting to arrest the alleged slayers of Sheriff Morris in Gonzales County, Sheriff R. M. Glover and Constable Henry Schnabel were killed and three Mexicans wounded.

June 15—At Ottine, one Mexican was killed while resisting arrest.

June 16—A Mexican was killed at Belmont and another wounded while resisting arrest.

June 17—A party of rangers near Benevides killed one Mexican, wounded another, and captured a third.

Total dead, six—three officers and three Mexicans. Wounded, Mexicans, six. Arrests so far as known, nine.

Manuel Cortez, the alleged slayer of Sheriffs Morris and Glover, it is said, is now within four miles of Cotulla, but has not yet been captured. Bloodhounds will be sent on his trail.

Figure 26 New York Times June 21, 1901

Meanwhile Cortez's wife Leonor and the children, Cortez's mother, and his sister-in-law María were illegally put in the Karnes City jail while posses mobilized to catch Cortez. On June 22, 1902 around noon on his twenty-sixth birthday Cortez walked into the sheep camp of Abrán de la Gárza. Jesús González, known as "El Teco." spotted Cortez and knew who he was. [246]

Gonzalez was either a good citizen or interested in the $1,000 reward contributed by the governor and the Karnes citizens. He quickly led Captain J. H. Rogers of the Texas Rangers and K. H. Merrem, a posse man, to the sheep camp. They got the drop on Cortez and arrested him before he could shoot his way out.

After his jailing in San Antonio a long legal battle fight began. The Miguel Hidalgo Workers' Society of San Antonio and other workers' organizations collected funds in Texas and Mexico. The end results of this large fund raising effort united the Tejano communities throughout South Texas.

Because of the hysteria over Morris's death in Karnes County, officials feared the citizens would hang him at the Karnes City jail ... so they wisely moved him to the jail in San Antonio.

Cortez was charged and tried separately for murdering the three lawmen. His trials were rarities in an era when any Mexican American accused of killing a Texas law officer stood little chance of living long enough to appear in court. [247]

When he was tried in Gonzales for killing Schnabel a deadlocked jury reduced the charge to second-degree murder before agreeing on a conviction. While he was in the Gonzales jail, a mob tried unsuccessfully to lynch him. He was transported to Karnes City where he was convicted and sentenced to death for murdering Morris. A third trial in Columbus, Texas ended with a life sentence for killing Glover.

However, the Texas Court of Criminal Appeals overturned all the verdicts. His last trial was in Corpus Christi in 1904 after which he began serving a life sentence. Efforts to have him pardoned began with his incarceration and finally succeeded in 1913 when Governor Oscar Colquitt issued him a conditional pardon. [248]

The story of Gregorio Cortez spread like wildfire from Karnes County to every Hispanic community in Texas and the Southwest in a very short time. What's amazing is that this was a time before the advent of radio, TV or the internet. Through word of mouth and the ubiquitous corrido or ballad, a form of folk song, his story went viral. [249]

Figure 27 Gregorio Cortez and Juan Mosqueda (aka Cipriano Rodriquez)- Courtesy Mosqueda family archives

These unique songs were highly stylized and in many cases romantic stories regarding the plight of Hispanic people along the Texas-Mexico border. One of the most famous corridos of the late nineteenth and twentieth century was the one from Karnes County. "El Corrido De Gregorio Cortez" was sung in ranch houses, homes and cantinas throughout South Texas.

When the Mexican Revolution gripped the north, Gregorio joined the Huerta forces but was wounded so he had to return to Manor, Texas. After he recovered he moved to Anson, Texas in 1916 where he died at the home of a friend at the age of forty-one. Gregorio Cortez is buried in a small cemetery eight miles outside of Anson. [250]

One thing we do know, Gregorio Cortez was a very resourceful man and until he was betrayed, he had outwitted and eluded hundreds of the best lawman in Texas.

Chapter 25: Today the Ghosts Roam Freely

Today the town of Helena is but a whispering ghost of her former self. The population has dwindled to less than 75 people. The remaining buildings from the 1860s and 1870s are sadly in need of repairs and restoration.

At night, under a black, star filled sky, sounds ricochet off old buildings like gunshots. The primary noises you hear are an occasional car stopping at one of the two rowdy saloons, mixed with the sound of barking dogs.

Although Helena is now a whispering ghost of her past greatness, occasionally she will give up a historical bone or two from her past life. In doing original historical research for this book, my sons and I have found some fascinating clues relating to day to day life in Old Helena. Here are just a few of the relics that allowed us, in a small way, to view a slice of life in old Helena: [251]

Figure 28 Civil War period 1860's Wine bottle ... may have been consumed before participation in the "Helena duel."

Figure 29 Merry Widows Condoms; Late 1800's, early 1900's Tin contained 3 condoms named Agnes, Mabel, and Beckie. Cost $1.00

Figure 30 Common Sense Item; Patent Date 1885-Could have been used as card cheating device for gamblers (Ace up your sleeve), in Helena's many saloons or as a cufflink ... if you got caught.

Figure 31 Safe Plate; 1850's-1860's R.M Patrick of New York City was the sole manufacture of these salamander safes. This one weighed about 700 lbs and could certainly hold a lot of gold and silver.

Figure 32 Lighter; Patent Date 1889-"Pocket Lamp" used for lighting cigars, lamps, gas burners, etc.

Figure 33 Silver Dime; 1838- 90% silver this clearly predates Helena and could be from the original Mexican village of Alamita, dating from the early to mid 1840's.

Figure 34 Texas saddle blanket ornament; mid 1800's, possibly used by Cavalry or Texas Rangers.

Today the old 1873 two story courthouse now serves as the Karnes County Museum. It overflows with an amazing amount of history. Old maps, pistols, photos and fascinating court records from the 1800's ... are just waiting to be discovered.

However one of the most interesting aspects of Helena is the secret that many of the remaining residents know but few will speak of. No, I'm not talking about the buried outlaw gold on treasure maps carried by suspicious looking visitors or the mysterious old records that had to be destroyed to avoid embarrassment.

What I'm talking about is the hidden truth that this ghost town is truly a ghost town. It is filled with an abundance of spirits and apparitions that have scared the hell out of the residents for well over a hundred years ... and continues to this very day.

The residents of this now tiny village know of what I speak: Strange fire balls, sounds, footsteps, shadows and voices: Floor fans stopping in the dead of the night ... as the electrical plug flies out of the wall socket and then crashes to the floor: Mother's seeing a shadow walking past a night light at midnight ... afraid to scream and wake their children: People pushed as they walk down the steps of the old courthouse.[252]

Ghostly figures from Old Helena touching adults or playing hide and go seek with two year olds, has become part of life in this town where so many died violently.

After much debate and concern the secret has been shared with some outsiders. Recently the San Antonio Paranormal Network (Associated with the popular Ghost Hunters TV show) was allowed access all night to the old courthouse, the Masonic Lodge and Mayfield store from the 1860s.

It was 4 a.m. on a bone chilling Sunday morning in November 2008 in the old ghost town of Helena, Texas. Under a very black night sky exploding with stars a small army of professional ghost hunters has just completed their second investigation of the town. They methodically disconnect and remove their sophisticated electronic equipment from the old buildings around the courthouse square.

Under the watchful eye of Robert Hernandez, founder of the San Antonio Paranormal Network (SAPN) and Case Manager Michelle Hernandez, the equipment is quickly loaded into a series of cars and vans. As this caravan begins its trek back to San Antonio the sound of their engines and lights quickly fade into silent darkness, only broken by the occasional howling coyote. This is Helena now ... but as you already know ... it wasn't always this way.

The first investigation of Helena by SAPN yielded an Electronic Voice Phenomena (EVP) recording in a small kitchen near the courthouse. On the recording the female investigator asked a question, Can you tell us why you're here? .... This was followed by a rapid (enhanced) response from an old man appearing to say "I know something"

The official report of this investigation given to Ramona Noone of the Karnes County Historical Society was essentially inconclusive. However, I do have a few personal observations as I was allowed to tag along to all the sites with this professional group of investigators. At one location, after an investigator asked some antagonistic questions to any spirits that may have been there, the temperature rose 20 degrees in just a few minutes. At a second location, I made similar unpleasant remarks, and we were all greeted with a heart-stopping loud crash at 3 a.m.

My other observation was that a number of pieces of the investigator's equipment, such as cameras, recorders, and walkie-talkies that had all been fully charged, kept discharging in these buildings. In one case the equipment only started to work again once they left the buildings under investigation ... which by the way had no electricity.

More recently in November 2010 an enhanced voice recorder was used late at night in the courthouse and a nearby building. There were four different EVP's recorded that night. The participants appeared quite upset at what they heard. You will have access to these EVP's on our web site at www.helenatexas.com.

As an electrical engineer, I tend to be skeptical of the paranormal however my new bottom line is ...don't mess with Helena's ghosts!!!

Notes

Chapter 1: The Beginning of the End

[1] Karnes County Historical Society "Welcome to old Helena."

[2] Interviews with Historian Robert Thonhoff.

[3] "THE KARNES AFFRAY; How the Two Men Met Their Deaths," The Daily Express, December 31, 1884.

[4] Ibid.

[5] "Wofford Crossing Road, "Maxine Yeater Linder, 1994, Kenedy City Library.

Chapter 2: The Beginning of the End

[6] Moon Austin, San Antonio, and the Hill Country by Justin Marler

[7] Handbook of Texas Online-Karnes County.

Chapter 3: The Europeans Are Coming

[8] Spanish Expeditions into Texas 1689-1768 by William C. Foster.

[9] Lonestar Genealogy-Immigration to Texas
http://www,lonestargenealogy.com/courses/texas/migration.html.

[10] Handbook of North American Indians, Volume 13 by William C. Sturtevant, Raymond J. DeMallie.

[11] "The Great Disease Migration" By Geoffrey Cowley "Newsweek" (Special Issue, Fall/Winter 1991, pp. 54-56."

[12] Notes of Spanish Colonial Historian, David J. Weber.

[13] Ibid.

[14] Ibid.

[15] Ibid.

Chapter 4: El Fuerte Del Cibolo

[16] The La Salle Expedition in Texas: The Journal of Henri Joutel, 1684-1687; Foster, William C., ed.; translated by Johanna S. Warren; Texas State Historical Association, Austin, 1998.

[17] Ibid.

[18] Ibid.

[19] Ibid.

[20] www.texasIndians.com, The Karankawa Indians By R. Edward Moore

[21] Ibid.

[22] Robert H. Thonhoff, El Fuerte del Cibolo: Sentinel of the Bexar-La Bahia Ranches (Austin: Eakin Press, 1992).

[23] Biography of CAPTAIN JOSE DE URRUTIA, Commander of the Royal Presidio of San Antonio de Bexar, By John D. Inclan, Edited by Bernadette Inclan.

[24] Ibid.

[25] Robert H. Thonhoff, El Fuerte del Cibolo: Sentinel of the Bexar-La Bahia Ranches (Austin: Eakin Press, 1992).

[26] Ibid.

[27] Ibid.

Chapter 5: The American Revolution and Texas

[28] The Texas Connection with The American Revolution, Robert H. Thonhoff, Eakin Press 2000.

[29] Ibid.

[30] Ibid.

[31] Forgotten Allies: Spains Aid During the American Revolution by Rudy Scott Nelson.

[32] Ibid.

[33] Ibid.

[34] Ibid.

[35] Ibid.

[36] Ibid.

[37] Ibid.

Chapter 6: The Battle of Medina

[38] Sons of Dewitt Colony, Texas © 1997-2007, Wallace L. McKeehan, Nueva España --Nuevas Philipinas—Provincia de Tejas

[39] Ibid.

[40] Green Flag Over Texas, By Julia Kathryn Garrett, Cordova Press, New York.

[41] Ibid.

[42] Handbook of Texas on Line, SANTA ANNA, ANTONIO LÓPEZ DE (1794–1876).

Chapter 7: The Anglo Invasion

[43] Cantrell, Gregg; Stephen F. Austin-Empesario of Texas; Yale University Press

[44] Ibid.

[45] Ibid.

[46] Ibid.

[47] The Texas Revolution; Brinkley, William; Texas A&M Press

[48] Ibid.

[49] Ibid.

Chapter 8: The Battle of the Alamo

[50] Handbook of Texas On Line, SANTA ANNA, ANTONIO LÓPEZ DE (1794–1876).

[51] Chariton, Wallace O. *100 Days in Texas: The Alamo Letters*. Plano, TX: Word-ware, 1990. Print

[52] Barr, Alwyn. Texans in Revolt, the Battle for San Antonio 1835. Austin, TX: University of Texas, 1990. Print.

[53] Handbook of Texas On Line, SANTA ANNA, ANTONIO LÓPEZ DE (1794–1876).

[54] Groneman, Bill. Eyewitness to the Alamo. Plano, TX: Republic of Texas, 1996. Print.

[55] Ibid.

[56] Ibid.

[57] Ibid.

[58] Ibid.

[59] Davis, William C.; Lone Star Rising-The Revolutionary Birth of the Texas Republic;Free Press

[60] Battle of san Jacinto-Handbook of Texas Online

[61] Ibid.

Chapter 9: Texas Is Now Free...But Not Free of Trouble

[62] Handbook of Texas On Line, The Republic of Texas

[63] William Campbell Binkley, The Expansionist Movement in Texas, 1836–1850 (Berkeley: University of California Press, 1925).

[64] Ibid.

[65] Swift, Roy L. Three Roads to Chihuahua. Print

[66] Ibid.

[67] Ibid.

[68] Ibid.

[69] M.L. Crimmins Map Collection, ECB.

[70] Swift, Roy L. Three Roads to Chihuahua. Print

[71] Ibid.

[72] Ibid.

[73] Smith, War with Mexico. And Crimmins, Wool in Texas.

[74] Swift, Roy L. Three Roads to Chihuahua. Print

Chapter 10: Helena and Karnes County Begin

[75] Didear, Hedwig K. A History of Karnes County and Old Helena. Austin, TX: San Felipe, 1969.

[76] Ibid.

[77] Ibid.

[78] Ibid.

[79] Ibid.

[80] Ibid.

[81] Ibid.

[82] Ibid.

[83] Advertisement for Helena lots for Sale, in the Western Texan April 11, 1854

[84]. Didear, Hedwig K. A History of Karnes County and Old Helena. Austin, Texas San Felipe, 1969.

[85] The Early History Of Panna Maria, Texas, Thomas Lindsay Baker, B.A

Chapter 11: The Early Years in Helena

[86] San Antonio Stage Lines 1847-1881, by Robert H. Thonhoff

[87] Ibid.

[88] Karnes County Historical Society. "Welcome to Old Helena" Print.

[89] Didear, Hedwig K. *A History of Karnes County and Old Helena*. Austin, TX: San Felipe, 1969.

[90] Ibid.

[91] The Karnes City Citation September 24, 1931.

Chapter 12: The Cortina Wars

[92] Rippy, J. F. "Border Troubles along the Rio Grande, 1848-1860" 23rd ed. 1919. Print.

[93] oldfinch, Charles W., and Jose T. Canales. Juan N. Cortina: Two Interpretations. New York: Arno, 1974. Print.

[94] Ibid.

[95] Ibid.

[96] Ibid.

[97] Ibid.

Chapter 13: The First Outlaws

[98] Didear, Hedwig K. A History of Karnes County and Old Helena. Austin, TX: San Felipe, 1969.

[99] Ibid.

[100] Ibid.

[101] Kilgore, Dan. "Two Sixshooters and a Sunbonnet: The Story of Sally Skull" Dallas, TX: E Heart, 1981. Print.

[102] Ibid.

[103] Ibid.

[104] Bradford, Virginia T. Sallie Scull on the Texas Frontier: Phantoms on Rio Turbio. San Antonio, TX: Naylor, 1952. Print.

[105] Ibid.

[106] Kilgore, Dan. "Two Sixshooters and a Sunbonnet: The Story of Sally Skull" Dallas, TX: E Heart, 1981. Print.

[107] Ibid.

Chapter 14: The Ox-Cart War

[108] Didear, Hedwig K. A History of Karnes County and Old Helena. Austin, TX: San Felipe, 1969. Print.

[109] Ibid.

[110] Ibid.

[111] Ibid.

[112] Ibid.

[113] Texas State Library & Archives Commission, Pease to the Texas Legislature, November 30, 1857.

Chapter 15: Knights Of the Golden Circle

[114] Stidger, Felix. Treason History, Order of Sons of Liberty, Knights of the Golden Circle, or American Knights 1864. 1903. Print.

[115] Bridges, C. A. (1941). "The Knights of the Golden Circle: A Filibustering Fantasy". Southwestern Historical Quarterly 44: 287–302.

[116] Ibid.

[117] Crenshaw, Ollinger (October 1941)." The Knights of the Golden Circle: The Career of George Bickley," American Historical Review.

[118] Dunn, Roy S. (April 1967). "The KGC in Texas, 1860-1861". Southwestern Historical Quarterly 70: 543–573.

[119] United States History: 1775 to 2000, A Manual for Students in HSTAA 101, Professor Quintard Taylor, Department of History, University of Washington, Fall 2004

[120] The Southwestern historical Quarterly, The K.G.C. in Texas, 1961-1865, Roy Sylvan Dunn.

[121] Stidger, Felix. Treason History, Order of Sons of Liberty, Knights of the Golden Circle, or American Knights 1864. 1903. Print.

[122] "Shadow of the Sentinel" by Warren Getler and Bob Brewer

[123] Ibid.

[124] Ibid.

[125] Stidger, Felix. Treason History, Order of Sons of Liberty, Knights of the Golden Circle, or American Knights 1864. 1903. Print.

[126] "Jesse James was One of His Names" by Del Schrader and Jesse James III

[127] "Shadow of the Sentinel" by Warren Getler and Bob Brewer

Chapter 16: The Civil War

[128] "Killing ground: photographs of the Civil War and the changing American landscape". John Huddleston (2002). Johns Hopkins University Press.

[129] The First Session of the Secession Convention of Texas, Anna Irene Sandbo, The Southwestern Historical Quarterly, vol. 18, No. 2 (Oct., 1914), pp. 162-194

[130] Duncan, "The book of Texas Lists," p 23

[131] Baum, Dale. The Shattering of Texas Unionism: Politics in the Lone Star State during the Civil War Era Louisiana State University Press, 1998

[132] The First Session of the Secession Convention of Texas, Anna Irene Sandbo, The Southwestern Historical Quarterly, vol. 18, No. 2 (Oct., 1914), pp. 162-194

[133] United States History: From 1775 to 2000, A Manual for Students in HSTAA 101, Professor Quintard Taylor, Department of History, University of Washington, Fall 2004

[134] Official Centennial Program, "Karnes County Centennial," May 5 ~ 9, 1954: and The Karnes County Story, Helmuth H. Schuenemann.

[135] Ibid.

[136] James Smallwood, "Disaffection in Confederate Texas: The Great Hanging at Gainesville," Civil War History 22 (December 1976) pp 349–60

[137] Ibid.

[138] Official Centennial Program, "Karnes County Centennial," May 5 ~ 9, 1954: The Karnes County Story, Helmuth H. Schuenemann.

[139] Petition No. 40, Citizens of Karnes County Ask that a Company be formed for the protection of Karnes and other counties, December 8, 1863 Texas State Archives, Austin, Texas.

[140]. Under the rebel flag, Life in Texas during the Civil War, From the Texas State Library and archives Commission.

[141] The Sutton-Taylor feud: the deadliest blood feud in Texas by Chuck Parsons 2009

[142] Clampitt, Brad R. "The Breakup: the Collapse of the Confederate Trans-Mississippi Army in Texas, 1865" Southwestern Historical Quarterly 2005

[143] The Last Battle of the Civil War Palmetto Ranch, By Jeffrey Wm Hunt

Chapter 17: Civil War Reconstruction

[144] Edward McPherson, The Political History of the United States of America During the Period of Reconstruction (1875).

[145] Ramsdell, Charles William. Reconstruction in Texas (19100

[146] Edward McPherson, The Political History of the United States of America During the Period of Reconstruction (1875).

[147] Vendetta, by Elmer Kelton

[148] Robert D. Marcus and David Burner, America Firsthand: From Reconstruction to the Present (New York: St. Martin's Press, 1989), p. 11.

[149] Reminiscences of Reconstruction in Texas; and reminiscences of Texas and Texans Fifty Years Ago by W.D. Wood 1902.

Chapter 18: Civil War Reconstruction In Kearnes County

[150] The First Polish Americans: Silesian Settlements in Texas.

[151] Didear, Hedwig K. A History of Karnes County and Old Helena. Austin, TX: San Felipe, 1969. Print.

[152] Robert H. Thonhoff, History of Karnes County, M.A. thesis, Southwest Texas State College, 1963.

[153] Bartholomew, Ed Ellsworth. Wild Bill Longley: A Texas Hard-Case, Frontier Press of Texas, Houston, 1953

[154] Ibid.

[155] Ibid.

[156] Ibid.

[157] Galveston News September 16, 1877.

[158] The First Polish Americans Find Hope in Texas, by Kathryn G. Rosypal

[159] The Early History Of Panna Maria, Texas, Thomas Lindsay Baker, B.A.

[160] Ibid.

[161] Ibid.

[162] Ibid.

[163] Ibid.

[164] Ibid.

[165] Ibid.

[166] Ibid.

[167] Ibid.

[168] Ibid.

[169] Ibid.

[170] Ibid.

[171] Ibid.

[172] Ibid.

[173] Otis, George A. A Report of Surgical Cases Treated in the Army of the United States From 1865-1871. Washington: Government Printing Office, 1871. Print.

[174] The Early History Of Panna Maria, Texas, Thomas Lindsay Baker, B.A.

[175] Ibid.

[176] Ibid.

[177] Ibid.

[178] The Karnes City Citation September 24, 1931.

[179] Texas State Library and Archives, Portraits of Texas Governors.

Chapter 19: The Taylor Gang

[180] Sons of DeWitt Colony, Dewitt Colonists 1828 Surnames, Taylor, Josiah.

[181] Ibid.

[182] Ibid.

[183] Ibid.

[184] Smallwood, James M. "The Feud That Wasn't" Texas A&M UP, 2008. Print.

[185] Ibid.

[186] Ibid.

[187] Ibid.

[188] Ibid.

[189] Ibid.

[190] Ibid.

[191] Parsons, Chuck. The Sutton-Taylor Feud: the Deadliest Blood Feud in Texas. Denton, TX: University of North Texas, 2009. Print.

[192] Ibid.

[193] Ibid.

[194] Ibid.

[195] Ibid.

Chapter 20: The Taylor-Sutton-John Wesley Hardin Feud

[196] Smallwood, James M. "The Feud That Wasn't" Texas A&M UP, 2008. Print.

[197] Ibid.

[198] Ibid.

[199] Ibid.

[200] Metz, Leon,(1996) John Wesley Hardin: Dark Angel of Texas," Mangan Books, El Paso, Texas

[201] Smallwood, James M. "The Feud That Wasn't" Texas A&M UP, 2008. Print.

[202] Ibid.

[203] Ibid.

Chapter 21: Helena Texas the Boom Town

[204] Didear, Hedwig K. A History of Karnes County and Old Helena. Austin, TX: San Felipe, 1969. Print.

[205] Ibid.

[206] Ibid.

[207] Ibid.

[208] Originally published in: Karnes County Centennial, Karnes City. Texas, May 5-9, 1954.

[209] Ibid.

[210] "Notes of the Week: Home and Abroad." The Christian Life [London] 3 July 1880, 6th ed. Print.

[211] Blackburn, Edward A. Wanted: Historic County Jails of Texas. TAMU, 2006. Print.

[212] Helena Bridge Company. By-laws of the Helena Bridge Company, Helena, Texas. Bickler & Lindheimer,1875. Print.

[213] Karnes County Historical Society. "Welcome to Old Helena" Print.

[214] From the Kenedy Advance April 15, 1926.

[215] January, 2002 issue of "The Kansas Cowboy".

Chapter 22: The Daileyville Massacre

[216] KARNES COUNTY TEXAS GUNFIGHTS, By Archie B. Ammons.

[217] Ibid.

[218] Ibid.

[219] Scudder, John M., ed. "Specific Medicines." The Eclectic Medical Journal 40 (1880). Print.

[220] KARNES COUNTY TEXAS GUNFIGHTS, By Archie B. Ammons.

[221] Ibid.

[222] Transcript of the inquest into the shootings at Daileyville.

[223] "Wofford Crossing Road," Maxine Yeater Linder, 1994, Kenedy City Library.

[224] Transcript of the inquest into the shootings at Daileyville.

[225] Ibid.

[226] Ibid.

[227] Ibid.

[228] Ibid.

[229] Ibid.

[230] San Antonio light, September 7, 1886.

[231] The Life and Death of Juan Coy, By Charles L. Olmsted and Edward Coy Ybarra.

[232] On site investigation by author Barry Harrin and sons Brian and Brandon Harrin.

Chapter 23: Helena's Painful Death

[233] 7 Jan 1894 San Antonio Express (21 Dec 1893) move County seat.

[234] Didear, Hedwig K. A History of Karnes County and Old Helena. Austin, TX: San Felipe, 1969. Print.

[235] Ibid.

[236] Ibid.

[237] Ibid.

[238] See Figure 36 Actual election results-Courtesy of the Karnes County Museum, Helena, Texas

[239] Didear, Hedwig K. A History of Karnes County and Old Helena. Austin, TX: San Felipe, 1969. Print.

Chapter 24: The Ballad of Gregorio Cortez

[240] Afterword by Bill Crider. Elmer Kelton. Manhunters. Texas Christian University Press, 1994.

[241] Paredes, Américo (1958). With His Pistol In His Hand. Austin: University of Texas Press

[242] Tales of bad men, bad women, and bad places: four centuries of Texas outlawry, By Charley F. Eckhardt.

[243] Paredes, Américo (1958). With His Pistol In His Hand. Austin: University of Texas Press

[244] Ibid.

[245] Ibid.

[246] Ibid.

[247] Ibid.

[248] Rosales, F. Arturo. Pobre Raza! Violence, Justice, and Mobilization among Mexico Lindo Immigrants, 1900-1936. Austin: University of Texas Press, 1999:

[249] Paredes, Américo (1958). With His Pistol In His Hand. Austin: University of Texas Press

[250] Ibid.

Chapter 25: Today the Ghosts Roam Freely

[251] A small sample of artifacts discovered in Helena, Texas by Brian and Brandon Harrin.

[252] Information provided to the author by many residents of Helena, Texas past and present.

Barry H. Harrin

Index

About the Author

Author Barry Harrin with his sons Brian and Brandon looking for trouble in Tombstone

Author Barry Harrin fought his way up from a gang infested section of New York City to the top of corporate America. He has worked in the immigrant slums of London, Paris, Brussels and Frankfurt in addition to the violent streets of Cairo, Johannesburg and Mexico City.

Barry is also the author of "A Manager's Guide to Guerrilla Warfare," Guess Who's Listening at the Other End of Your Telephone," and "The Islamic Conquest of Europe 2020."

He has been featured in articles or news stories by the Associated Press, LaSoir (Brussels, Belgium), Dallas Times Herald, Houston Post and Success Magazine to name a few.

He has conducted business training seminars and been interviewed on television and talk radio shows across America and Europe.

During the Vietnam Period, Barry served in the United States Naval Air Force as a Combat Air Crewman. Barry is a former kick-boxer, and telecommunications entrepreneur.

Barry's best-selling book "A Manager's Guide to Guerrilla Warfare," was chosen by the United States Air Force-Patrick AFB Library System, as one of the top leadership and management books of all time.

CPSIA information can be obtained at www.ICGtesting.com
Printed in the USA
BVOW06s1106171115

427457BV00024B/433/P